CliffsNotes™ Setting Up a Windows® 98 Home Network

By Sue Plumley

IN THIS BOOK

- Find out what a home computer network can do for you
- Get the lowdown on networking hardware and software
- Decide which home networking options are best for you
- Reinforce what you learn with CliffsNotes Review
- Find more information about home computer networking in the CliffsNotes Resource Center and online at www.cliffsnotes.com

IDG Books Worldwide, Inc.
An International Data Group Company
Foster City, CA • Chicago, IL • Indianapolis, IN • New York, NY

About the Author
Sue Plumley has owned and operated her own computer consulting business since 1988. In addition to her business, Sue has also authored 36 computer books and co-authored another 35 books for Que, John Wiley and Sons, Inc., IDG Books Worldwide, Inc., DDC, and other publishers.

Publisher's Acknowledgments
Editorial
Project Editor: Paul Levesque
Acquisitions Editor: Joyce Pepple
Copy Editor: James Russell
Technical Editor: Eric Butow

Production
Indexer: York Production Services, Inc.
Proofreader: York Production Services, Inc.
IDG Books Indianapolis Production Department

CliffsNotes™ Setting Up a Windows® 98 Home Network
Published by
IDG Books Worldwide, Inc.
An International Data Group Company
919 E. Hillsdale Blvd.
Suite 400
Foster City, CA 94404
www.idgbooks.com (IDG Books Worldwide Web site)
www.cliffsnotes.com (CliffsNotes Web site)

Note: If you purchased this book without a cover you should be aware that this book is stolen property. It was reported as "unsold and destroyed" to the publisher, and neither the author nor the publisher has received any payment for this "stripped book."

Copyright © 2000 IDG Books Worldwide, Inc. All rights reserved. No part of this book, including interior design, cover design, and icons, may be reproduced or transmitted in any form, by any means (electronic, photocopying, recording, or otherwise) without the prior written permission of the publisher.
Library of Congress Catalog Card No.: 99-66717
ISBN: 0-7645-8541-X
Printed in the United States of America
10 9 8 7 6 5 4 3 2 1
1O/RZ/RR/ZZ/IN
Distributed in the United States by IDG Books Worldwide, Inc.
Distributed by CDG Books Canada Inc. for Canada; by Transworld Publishers Limited in the United Kingdom; by IDG Norge Books for Norway; by IDG Sweden Books for Sweden; by IDG Books Australia Publishing Corporation Pty. Ltd. for Australia and New Zealand; by TransQuest Publishers Pte Ltd. for Singapore, Malaysia, Thailand, Indonesia, and Hong Kong; by Gotop Information Inc. for Taiwan; by ICG Muse, Inc. for Japan; by Intersoft for South Africa; by Eyrolles for France; by International Thomson Publishing for Germany, Austria and Switzerland; by Distribuidora Cuspide for Argentina; by LR International for Brazil; by Galileo Libros for Chile; by Ediciones ZETA S.C.R. Ltda. for Peru; by WS Computer Publishing Corporation, Inc., for the Philippines; by Contemporanea de Ediciones for Venezuela; by Express Computer Distributors for the Caribbean and West Indies; by Micronesia Media Distributor, Inc. for Micronesia; by Chips Computadoras S.A. de C.V. for Mexico; by Editorial Norma de Panama S.A. for Panama; by American Bookshops for Finland.
For general information on IDG Books Worldwide's books in the U.S., please call our Consumer Customer Service department at **800-762-2974**. For reseller information, including discounts and premium sales, please call our Reseller Customer Service department at **800-434-3422**.
For information on where to purchase IDG Books Worldwide's books outside the U.S., please contact our International Sales department at 317-596-5530 or fax **317-596-5692**.
For consumer information on foreign language translations, please contact our Customer Service department at **1-800-434-3422**, fax **317-596-5692**, or e-mail rights@idgbooks.com.
For information on licensing foreign or domestic rights, please phone +1-650-655-3109.
For sales inquiries and special prices for bulk quantities, please contact our Sales department at 650-655-3200 or write to the address above.
For information on using IDG Books Worldwide's books in the classroom or for ordering examination copies, please contact our Educational Sales department at **800-434-2086** or fax **317-596-5499**.
For press review copies, author interviews, or other publicity information, please contact our Public Relations department at **650-655-3000** or fax **650-655-3299**.
For authorization to photocopy items for corporate, personal, or educational use, please contact Copyright Clearance Center, 222 Rosewood Drive, Danvers, MA 01923, or fax **978-750-4470**.

LIMIT OF LIABILITY/DISCLAIMER OF WARRANTY: THE PUBLISHER AND AUTHOR HAVE USED THEIR BEST EFFORTS IN PREPARING THIS BOOK. THE PUBLISHER AND AUTHOR MAKE NO REPRESENTATIONS OR WARRANTIES WITH RESPECT TO THE ACCURACY OR COMPLETENESS OF THE CONTENTS OF THIS BOOK AND SPECIFICALLY DISCLAIM ANY IMPLIED WARRANTIES OF MERCHANTABILITY OR FITNESS FOR A PARTICULAR PURPOSE. THERE ARE NO WARRANTIES WHICH EXTEND BEYOND THE DESCRIPTIONS CONTAINED IN THIS PARAGRAPH. NO WARRANTY MAY BE CREATED OR EXTENDED BY SALES REPRESENTATIVES OR WRITTEN SALES MATERIALS. THE ACCURACY AND COMPLETENESS OF THE INFORMATION PROVIDED HEREIN AND THE OPINIONS STATED HEREIN ARE NOT GUARANTEED OR WARRANTED TO PRODUCE ANY PARTICULAR RESULTS, AND THE ADVICE AND STRATEGIES CONTAINED HEREIN MAY NOT BE SUITABLE FOR EVERY INDIVIDUAL. NEITHER THE PUBLISHER NOR AUTHOR SHALL BE LIABLE FOR ANY LOSS OF PROFIT OR ANY OTHER COMMERCIAL DAMAGES, INCLUDING BUT NOT LIMITED TO SPECIAL, INCIDENTAL, CONSEQUENTIAL, OR OTHER DAMAGES.

Trademarks: Cliffs, CliffsNotes, and all related logos and trade dress are registered trademarks or trademarks of Cliffs Notes, Inc. in the United States and other countries. All other brand names and product names used in this book are trade names, service marks, trademarks, or registered trademarks of their respective owners. IDG Books Worldwide, Inc. and Cliffs Notes, Inc. are not associated with any product or vendor mentioned in this book.

 is a registered trademark under exclusive license to IDG Books Worldwide, Inc. from International Data Group, Inc.

Table of Contents

Introduction **1**
   Why Do You Need This Book? 1
   How to Use This Book 2
   Don't Miss Our Web Site 3

Chapter 1: Understanding the Network **5**
   Peer-to-Peer Networking 6
   Planning Your Network 9
   Putting Your Computer's House in Order 11
   Understanding Networked Programs 13
      Using networked programs 14
      Understanding licensing 15
      Storing shared files 16

Chapter 2: Choosing Network Equipment **17**
   Choosing Kits 17
      Phone line kits 19
      Traditional cabling kits 20
      Wireless kits 21
   Buying and Installing Network Cards 22
      Buying a network card 22
      Installing a network card 24
   Buying and Installing a Hub 26

Chapter 3: Connecting Your Network **28**
   Connecting Only Two Computers 28
      DCC cable 29
      Installing DCC 29
      Configuring DCC and connecting DCC cable 30
      Configuring Windows 98 32
      Running the direct cable connection 33
   Connecting with Traditional Cabling 34
      Examining the cable 34
      Installing the cable 35
   Using Phone Lines to Connect 37
   Using Wireless Connections 38

Chapter 4: Setting Up the Computers 39
Installing and Configuring the Network Interface Card Software 39
    Installing the NIC software 40
    Configuring the NIC software 44
Windows 98's Built-In Client Software 45
Network Protocols 46
    Installing a protocol 47
    Configuring TCP/IP 48
Setting Services 50
Identifying the Computer 51
Exploring Access Control 53

Chapter 5: Sharing Folders, Drives, Files, and Internet Access 55
Understanding Sharing and Access Limits 56
    Access types 56
    Share designation 56
Sharing Folders, Drives, and Files 57
    Identifying folders to share 57
    Designating a shared folder 59
    Designating a shared drive 61
    Designating a file as shared 62
Sharing Internet Access 63
    Using third-party applications 63
    Software options 64

Chapter 6: Getting on (And around) the Network 66
Logging On and Off 66
    Looking at usernames 67
    Considering passwords 67
    Logging off of the network 68
Using Network Paths to Find Folders and Files 68
Mapping Drives 70
    Accessing a mapped drive 72
    Disconnecting a mapped drive 72
Applying Quick Logon 73
Finding Computers on the Network 75
    Finding a computer 75
    Finding a networked folder 77

Chapter 7: Using the Network Neighborhood 78
Browsing the Network Neighborhood 78
Working with Files and Folders 80
   Finding files 81
   Creating a shortcut 82
   Creating, deleting, and renaming files and folders 83
   Copying and moving files and folders 83

Chapter 8: Printing on the Network 85
Sharing a Printer 85
Installing and Configuring a Network Printer 87
   Installing a network printer 87
   Configuring the printer 89
Capturing a Printer Port 91
Managing the Printer 92
   Using the print queue 92
Optimizing Print Resources 96

Chapter 9: Managing the Network 97
Understanding Network Management 97
Using NetWatcher 99
   Configuring the computer for NetWatcher 99
   Starting and quitting NetWatcher 100
   Selecting a server 101
   Disconnecting a user 103
   Closing a file 103
   Working with shared folders 104
Using WinPopup 105
   Locating WinPopup 105
   Sending messages 105
   Receiving messages 107
   Changing options 107

CliffsNotes Review 109

CliffsNotes Resource Center 112
Books 112
Internet 113
Checklist 115
Send Us Your Favorite Tips 116

Index 117

INTRODUCTION

A significant number of homes today have at least one computer, and a good percentage of those homes have two or more. Given the appeal of the newer computer technologies, you may have already found yourself in situations where some family strife has broken out over the issue of who gets to use a particular computer, program, or printer — and when. How often have you found yourself muttering under your breath, "There must be a better way!"

I'm here to tell you that there is a better way. Businesses have used networks to share files, printers, applications, and other resources for years. Business owners and managers know the value of sharing information and collaborating on projects. If you have two or more computers in your home, you can take advantage of networking as well.

Use CliffsNotes *Setting Up a Windows 98 Home Network* to find out how a network can work for you. Reference the book when you're purchasing your network equipment and use it when you're sitting at your computer trying to print to another computer on the network. Find definitions and terminology, instructions for using Windows 98 on a network, and advice for getting the most out of your computers with CliffsNotes *Setting Up a Windows 98 Home Network*.

Why Do You Need This Book?

Can you answer yes to any of these questions?

- Do you need to learn about sharing your printer with your spouse fast?
- Do you not have the time to read 500 pages on cable and network interface cards?

- Do you want information about how to install networking hardware and software?
- Do you want to know how two members of your family can share an Internet account?
- Do you want to save money when buying expensive equipment, such as printers, hard drives, and CD-ROM drives?

If so, then CliffsNotes *Setting Up a Windows 98 Home Network* is for you!

How to Use This Book

You're the boss here. You get to decide how to use this book. You can either read the book from cover to cover or just look for the information you want and put it back on the shelf for later.

You can find information on a particular topic in a number of ways: You can search the index in the back of the book, locate your topic in the Table of Contents, or scan the In This Chapter list in each chapter. To reinforce what you learn, check out the Review and the Resource Center at the back of the book. To help you find important information in the book, look for the following icons in the text:

The Warning icon alerts you to something that could be dangerous, requires special caution, or should be avoided.

If you see a Tip icon, you'll know that you've run across a helpful hint, uncovered a secret, or received helpful advice.

 If you see a Remember icon, make a mental note, because this text is worth keeping in mind.

Don't Miss Our Web Site

Keep up with the changing world of home computer networks by visiting our Web site at www.cliffsnotes.com. Here's what you'll find:

- Interactive tools that are fun and informative
- Links to interesting Web sites
- Additional resources to help you continue your learning

At www.cliffsnotes.com, you can even register for a new feature called CliffsNotes Daily, which offers you newsletters on a variety of topics, delivered right to your e-mail inbox each business day.

If you haven't discovered the Internet and are wondering how to get online, pick up CliffsNotes *Getting On the Internet*. You'll learn just what you need to make your online connection quickly and easily. See you at www.cliffsnotes.com!

CHAPTER 1
UNDERSTANDING THE NETWORK

IN THIS CHAPTER

- Why a computer network?
- Defining your goals
- Planning your network
- Considering computer contents

You may be wondering why anyone would be interested in setting up their own computer network. If you have two or more computers in your home, you can *network*, or connect, the computers together so that you can share files, disk space, Internet access, and more with any number of other individuals in your family. Imagine being able to print using the printer connected to the computer a couple of bedrooms down without even leaving your desk or using one computer to send e-mail via the Internet while your teenager is busily surfing the Web on another computer, all the while using the same modem, Internet connection, and Internet account. An efficient home network can save you money by letting you share expensive equipment like printers and CD-ROM drives with other members of your family.

The benefits seem pretty obvious, but you may be concerned that setting up a home computer network can end up being a rather complicated affair. The sections in this chapter show you that setting up a home network is not at all as complicated as it sounds, once you understand some of the basics of computer networking.

Peer-to-Peer Networking

Usually when people speak of a home computer network, they are referring to a *peer-to-peer network,* the most common type of home computer network. So-called *client/server networks,* where one powerful computer provides resources to other less-powerful computers, do offer an alternative networking method, but they are typically found in business situations where more than ten computers are networked. For the purposes of home computer networking, then, peer-to-peer networks are the more practical solution.

Now, in a jury of one's peers, everybody is equal to everybody else. The same principle applies to a peer-to-peer network, where all computers are on a level playing field in terms of their participation in the network. Each computer can still work alone — run its own programs, save files, print (if it has a printer attached), run a CD-ROM (if it has a CD-ROM drive) — but, with the help of a bit of cable, some software, and a few connections, each computer now has access to the other computers on the peer-to-peer network and can share its resources with the others. Resources include the following:

- **Files**. With the appropriate permissions, you can open or copy a file that is located on another computer on the network. You can work on the file, print it, save it, and even delete that file as if it were your own. Other people working on the network can also open files on your computer. For more on permissions, see Chapter 5.

- **Folders**. Use folders, or directories, on other computers to store your files or to find other users' files.

- **Hard drives**. You can use any networked computer's hard drive to open someone's files and folders or to store your own files and folders.

Chapter 1: Understanding the Network

- **CD-ROM drives**. Use the CD-ROM drive on a networked computer to install programs on your own computer or to copy or open files from a CD.

- **Printers**. Sharing printers is one of the biggest advantages of networking your home computers. You may have only one fancy laser or color inkjet printer. Without a network, only one lucky person gets to use it. If, however, you network your computers, you can share that one printer with everyone on the network.

Figure 1-1 illustrates an example of a peer-to-peer network. The Windows 98 computers are connected to each other. The laser printer is connected to one computer, but everyone on the network can use it.

Figure 1-1: Three computers share their resources.

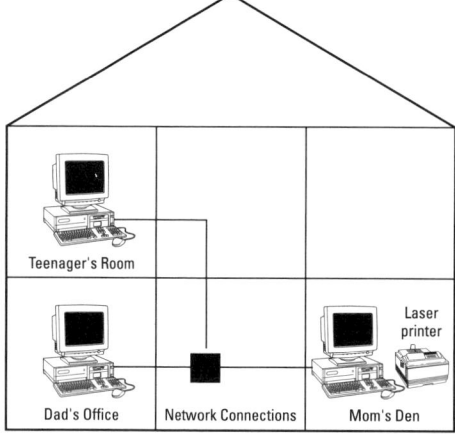

Defining Your Goals

Set network goals to help determine what networking hardware and software you'll use to build your system. You must consider equipment expense, network speed, the layout of the network, and your family's use of the network. Take an inventory of your current hardware and determine what equipment is viable for network use and what equipment you may want to replace.

Consider the following when planning your networking goals:

- Find out the programs each person wants to run. Check the minimum requirements of these programs and make sure that each computer has the power, memory, hard disk space, and other necessities to run the programs needed. Also, ask what types of programs the users will want for the future.

- Decide which tasks you want to perform on the network — sharing files and folders, sharing a printer or Internet access, playing network games, transferring music files, and so on.

- Think about how much money you want to spend on the network. With the available networking equipment and software, you can spend anywhere between $25 and $15,000 on a home network. The amount of money you spend depends on several things: how important the network is in your family's life, how much you will use the network each day, and what results you want from the network.

- Consider all the nice extras you have attached to your computer (technically referred to as *peripherals*): printers, CD-ROM drives, Iomega Zip drives, modems, and so on. You can share all of this equipment over the network, but you have to make sure that each piece will be able to handle the extra use that comes with being on a network.

Planning Your Network

In planning your network, make sure that each individual computer is in good shape before putting it on a network. You may even consider upgrading some of the features of your computers by adding memory or an extra hard drive or by changing operating systems. Next, decide which *resources* (printers, CD-ROM drives, hard drives, and so on) need to stay on which computer. Finally, decide where to locate each computer and each piece of peripheral equipment before continuing to plan your network.

You may also want to keep a summary sheet, or a needs list, of hardware and software. As you decide the type of networking hardware and software you'll be using, keep a list of what you need. Check each computer to make sure it meets the minimum hardware and software requirements for each software application or networking extra you add. The packaging on most software applications or hardware extras you buy usually lists the minimum system requirements to use them effectively. Remember that "minimum" often means "bare minimum." If you really want your software applications and hardware extras to run properly, make sure your computer has more than just the bare minimum.

Think about how the network will be laid out in your home. Decide where you will place the fastest computer, where the printer(s) will be located, whether two or more computers can be placed in the same room, and so on. Draw a *network map,* or a sketch of where in the home each computer and peripheral will be located. As you build your network, you can add information about the cabling and networking hardware and other information that will help you add to the network, make repairs, and troubleshoot problems later. List the specifications and programs for each computer. Figure 1-2 shows a sample network map.

Figure 1-2: Use a map to describe the network.

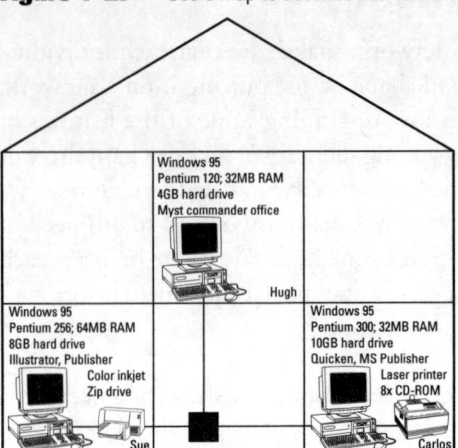

Looking at Networking Hardware

When you have your plan in place, your next step involves purchasing the right kind of networking equipment. In general, you need the following:

- Network interface card (NIC) for each computer on the network. A *NIC* (pronounced "nick") is a card that plugs into the computer and works to control the flow of information over the network. Each NIC connects to networking cable, which in turn connects to the other NICs on the network to create paths of communication.

- *Cables* are wires that connect the network cards and computers. You can choose from various types of cables; you can even make network connections using radio frequencies instead of cabling. See Chapter 2 for more information on cables.

- Depending on the type of network you use, you'll need either a network hub, your house's phone jacks, or a set of transmitters and receivers. A *network hub* is a centrally located device into which you plug all network cables, a kind of central meeting place for connecting and enabling communication over the network. You use the phone jacks in your home with a different type of network, where your house's phone lines act as the cables for your network. Transmitters and receivers represent yet another network type where radio frequencies, rather than cables, are used to communicate between computers. See Chapter 2 for more information.

Putting Your Computer's House in Order

Before you set up a network, consider how each computer uses Windows 98 to keep track of its resources and how each tracking method may affect the other network users. Each network user on a peer-to-peer network can view and use resources from computers other than his or her own. You want to make it easy for the users to find files, folders, printers, and other resources on the network. Be sure that all users are familiar with the My Computer, Windows Explorer, and Network Neighborhood features in Windows 98. They are invaluable for keeping track of your resources on the network.

Network users can view and use shared folders and files on other network computers, so you want to create a system for naming files and folders that makes sense to everyone concerned and makes it easy for people to find what they need.

Although certain folders already exist on each computer, you can always add folders that represent specific files, users, and so on. You can create any number of folders to hold your own data, games, and backup files. When creating folders, make sure you name the folders so that they are easily recognizable.

Leave folders that already exist — such as the Windows folder, Program Files, other application folders, and so on — exactly as they are. Never change the name or location of these folders. If you change the name of the Windows folder, for example, the operating system will no longer work.

Consider the following naming guidelines when adding folders to your network:

- Long folder names can be difficult to read when viewed in certain windows, such as in the Find Files and Folders dialog box. You end up losing half the folder name. To name a folder Letters to David About College, for example, probably isn't smart. Instead, you could name the folder David College or simply College.

- Keep filenames and folder names consistent. Consider prefacing each folder name or filename with the name of the family member who created it, such as SUE CHAPTER1, SUE CHAPTER2, HUGH REPORT1, and HUGH REPORT2. Things go a lot quicker if filenames and folder names give you as much consistent information as possible about what they contain.

- The My Computer, Windows Explorer, and Network Neighborhood features of Windows 98 list filenames and folder names alphabetically. Keep this in mind when trying to find a file or folder in a long list of files and folders.

- Folder names that begin with a number are listed in numerical order and come before all alphabetized folder names. For example, a folder named 98 Budget not only precedes one named 99 Budget, it also precedes one entitled simply Budget.

- Folder names that begin with a symbol are listed before numbered names in this order: #, $, %, &, @.

Chapter 1: Understanding the Network   **13**

You can place files in folders named after individual users or specific document types (letters, reports, and so on) or place one user folder inside of another folder (called *nesting*). C:\Documents\Sue is an example of nested folders where the Sue folder is nested within the Documents folder, just like those cute wooden Russian nesting dolls where one little wooden doll is hidden within a larger doll that is in turn hidden within a larger doll and so on.

Just as you plan how you name your shared folders, you should also plan how to name your files. The rules for file naming are similar to those for folders: Files list in alphabetical order, filenames beginning with a number precede those beginning with a letter, and filenames beginning with a symbol precede numbered names.

With filenames, you also have the added luxury of identifying files by using *extensions* (the .doc, .xls, .bmp, or .tif that is automatically added to the filenames of the Word documents, Excel spreadsheets, or image files you create). File extensions make it easier to sort filenames and find the file you want. You immediately know which files are word processing files, which are graphics files, and which are spreadsheet files.

You can see all filename extensions in the Windows Explorer window by choosing View➪Folder Options➪View Tab. Remove the check mark from the Hide File Extensions for Known File Types option.

Understanding Networked Programs

When planning how best to use your various computer programs across your network, ask yourself these questions:

- What are the system requirements for each program?
- What are the legal issues involved in using multiple copies of a program?
- Which computer on the network is best suited to store all the shared data from multiple users?

Using networked programs

When working on a peer-to-peer network, you still need to install your programs on each computer. By now you know that a network allows you to share files, but it's important to remember that accessing a shared file from another computer on the network does you no good if you don't have the program necessary to read that file on your own computer. This limitation is why making sure that all the computers on your network can meet the system requirements for a particular program is important. If you can't install a program on one of your computers on the network because the computer doesn't meet the minimum system requirements, you're out of luck. The computer can't "borrow" memory or hard drive space for installing a program from another computer on the network.

Using a program on a network comes with its own special quirks. Users can share the files created from any program (as long as the user's computer has the necessary program installed), but no two users can open the same file at the same time. If one person is using a file — a word processing, spreadsheet, accounting, or other file — and someone else tries to open that same file, a warning dialog box appears. The dialog box states that the file is already in use and asks if the user wants to make a copy of the file. This safeguard ensures that two users won't unwittingly try to edit the same file at the same time.

Certain networkable programs — games, for example — are specifically designed to let two or more people play the game at the same time. Other networkable applications — databases and accounting programs, for example — also try to protect open files, but they take a different approach. These types of programs let two or more people open the same file, but only the person who opened the file first is actually allowed to make any changes to the file. The second person is locked out from making any changes and has to be content with just reading the file.

Understanding licensing

Word processors, spreadsheets, drawing programs, and many games are licensed to one user only. You install these applications to your computer, and only you are licensed to use them. Licensing agreements are issued by the manufacturer and state the legal uses of programs.

Some manufacturers produce network versions of their applications. You can install these programs on multiple machines, depending on the number of licenses you own. Network versions of applications have built-in features that make them efficient and effective over the network. They also contain features that protect the data when in use by more than one person.

You might network a calendar or scheduling program, for instance, or an accounting program, a database, or a multi-user game. When purchasing an application, make sure you check to see if it's a network version and find out about the licensing as well.

Storing shared files

Determine where you will store the data that two or more network users use. Store the data on the most powerful computer you have — the one with the most powerful processor, the largest hard disk, and the most memory — so it can efficiently handle the increased demands that will necessarily come with more people trying to access the same resources. For example, a computer with a 10GB hard drive will store more data for the network than a computer with only a 2GB hard drive. A computer with a 350 MHz processor and 64MB of RAM can more quickly open and copy files than a computer with only a 190 MHz processor and 32MB of RAM.

Also, choose a computer that will be turned on most of the time, because people will need access to the computer to retrieve data.

CHAPTER 2
CHOOSING NETWORK EQUIPMENT

IN THIS CHAPTER

- Choosing kits
- Buying and installing network cards
- Buying and installing a hub

Choosing your network hardware may seem like a daunting task, but it's easier than you think. Many manufacturers make kits for home networking, complete with instructions and all the equipment you need. Alternatively, you can buy network cards and other equipment separately to put together your own networking configuration.

Choosing Kits

You can hire someone — a computer technician or consultant, for example — to install your networking equipment, or you can do it yourself. The easiest way to buy and install networking equipment is to buy a networking kit. Starter kits usually contain everything you need to connect the first two computers, and then you can buy any additional equipment you need for connecting more computers to the network.

Make sure you buy your kit from a reputable company. Some companies that make networking kits include Linksys, 3Com, NetGear, and D-Link.

Networking kits include the following:

- Network cards (also called network interface cards or network adapter cards), which are similar to other cards in your computer — such as sound or video cards. A printed electronic circuit board that snaps into an empty slot inside of the computer, the network card connects to a network cable from the back of the computer.

- Network cabling, which is the electronic wiring that connects one computer to another in the network. Cabling also connects printers to the network.

- Networking hardware, which includes the different kinds of equipment you use to complete a network. Depending on the kind of network you choose, you may need different kinds of hardware. See Chapter 3 for more information on networking hardware.

When you buy additional equipment to add to your existing network, you must buy the same type of cards and cabling. See Chapter 3 for more information.

Different networking kits are designed for different types of networks. The type of network you choose depends on how much money you want to spend and how fast you want the network to transfer data between computers. The three types of network kits suitable for home and small business networks are phone line kits, traditional cabling kits, and wireless kits.

Comparing the speed of various types of available networking technologies, one can say that phone line networks run at the speed of a skateboard, Ethernet networks (a particular kind of hubbed network) run at the speed of a race car, and Fast Ethernet (a high-end hubbed network) runs like a jet plane. Wireless methods can run at the speed of either the skateboard or the race car.

Phone line kits

You may want to explore using your telephone wiring for networking your computers together. When you use phone lines, you don't have to install any extra cabling. Phone line kits include networking cards and extra phone cable for connecting each computer to a wall jack.

Phone line networks do run slowly, however. The standard speed for moving data around on a phone line network is 1 megabit per second (or 1 Mbps). If you consider that 1 Mbps is twenty times faster than a 56 kilobits per second (Kbps) modem, it sounds pretty fast. But remember how slowly even a 56 Kbps modem downloads files.

Phone line networks are, however, fast enough for general networking, such as sharing small files or printers. If you want to use large graphic files or perform complex calculations regularly over the network, consider a faster networking technology.

Following are some other facts to consider about phone line networks:

- An organization called the HomePNA (Home Phoneline Networking Alliance) works to ensure that all phone line products adhere to certain standards so you're sure to get good quality and reliable service from phone line networking products.

- A phone line network can withstand high levels of atmospheric interference (lightning strikes) as well as signal noise from appliances, heaters, and other devices in the home (such as when your refrigerator or furnace kicks on).

- You don't need any other networking hardware when you use a phone line network.

Traditional cabling kits

Traditional cabling is called Ethernet. With Ethernet networking, speeds run at either 10 or 100 Mbps. If a network card or cabling is labeled simply "Ethernet," you can be pretty sure that it will run at only 10 Mbps. To earn the label "Fast Ethernet," a piece of equipment must be able to run at 100 Mbps.

Fast Ethernet isn't something you need for most home networking. Because it's more expensive to install and purchase, Fast Ethernet is better suited to businesses.

Ethernet cabling comes in various types for various sizes of networks. If you're putting in a home or small business network, be sure to use Category 5 UTP (Unshielded Twisted Pair) cabling. This type of cable provides a good quality network cable that is protected from interference and noise, is reliable, and is fairly inexpensive.

Following are some other facts to consider about Ethernet cabling networks:

- If you connect more than two computers with Ethernet cabling, you must use a *hub* (a special piece of networking hardware) as a central connecting device.

- The Ethernet kit includes the cable you need, plus the connectors for attaching the cable to a network card and to the hub.

- When you buy equipment for adding your third, fourth, or fifth computer to the network, you can buy cable in pre-made segments of 6-, 10-, 15-, 50-, and 100-foot sections. You need to buy a network cable and Ethernet card for each new computer.

- Hubs include four, six, eight, or more ports (plugs in which to connect the cables from each computer). Make sure that your hub has enough ports for the number of computers you plan to network. Plan for the future, as well. You may decide to add a computer or two to your network later, so buy a hub with the number of ports you need plus one or two extra.

- Ethernet cabling doesn't pick up atmospheric or other interference or noise.

- Ethernet kits cost more than phone line kits, but the speed difference may be worth the increase in cost to you.

Wireless kits

Wireless connections use radio signals or infrared beams to connect computers in a network rather than traditional cabling or phone lines. Wireless connections vary from speeds of 1 Mbps to 10 Mbps, depending on the wireless method.

Manufacturers have created wireless network cards, printer connections, and more for use with both desktop computers and portable (notebook or laptop) computers. Wireless kits are a bit more expensive than traditional cabling or phone line kits, but they can be used in your home safely and successfully. You may want to use wireless connections in your home if, for example, your walls are concrete. You cannot easily penetrate concrete walls to run cabling, but wireless works well in this situation.

Consider the following facts when thinking about using wireless networking:

- Wireless methods are easy to install and use. All you need is a network card and wireless port for each computer. The port enables the transmissions to move from one computer to another.

CliffsNotes Setting Up a Windows 98 Home Network

- Wireless provides more mobility for portable computers and users.

- The reliability of the connection is always questionable. Atmospheric conditions and obstacles, such as walls or ceilings, can cause the network connection to be less predictable than other networking technologies.

- Currently, wireless networks do run slower than most networks with traditional cabling (although some wireless networks are faster than phone line networks).

- Wireless is more expensive than traditional wiring methods.

Wireless connection methods are commonly used in combination with traditional cabling methods. You may want to use traditional cabling for the majority of your network and add a few wireless connections where appropriate, such as for someone using a notebook computer.

Buying and Installing Network Cards

A network card must match the slots for adapter cards in your computer. In addition to choosing the right card for your expansion slots, you want to think about price, brand, warranty, and the type of connectors on the card.

When you purchase a networking kit, the network card and cabling come with it, so you're sure you have the right connectors. Installing the card is fairly easy after you pick out the right one.

Buying a network card

The network card needs to fit the available expansion slots in your computer. Expansion slots are located inside your computer, near the back. These slots let you plug in cards or other devices to expand the usefulness of your computer.

Chapter 2: Choosing Network Equipment   **23**

Every computer has a limited number of expansion slots. Often, when you buy a computer, most or all of these slots are already in use. Look to make sure you have a slot open for a network card and to find out what type of slots you have.

The two most common slots for network cards are known as *ISA* (short for Industry Standard Architecture) and *PCI* (short for Peripheral Component Interconnect). Many computers have both types of slots. If you have a choice, choose a PCI for better communications, greater speed, and more efficiency in your network connections.

If you're using a portable computer, you'll need a different kind of card — a PCMCIA (Personal Computer Memory Card International Association) card — to fit the available slot in the smaller computer. PCMCIA cards are about the size of a credit card, and there are three types. Read your documentation to find out the type of card you can use with your computer.

In addition, consider the following information when buying a network card:

- Match the type of cabling you're using: phone line, Ethernet, or wireless. The card must specifically name the networking technology to work.

- Match the end connectors on your cabling to the connector on the network card. For example, if your cabling is phone line, make sure that the network card has a plug that works with a phone jack.

- Most network cards cost about the same, but avoid any cards that are considerably cheaper than others; these may be obsolete or damaged.

- Warranties range from a few months to a lifetime warranty. Because it's a buyer's market (there are so many cards from which to choose and competition is fierce), always get a card with a lifetime warranty.

- Use a known company with a good reputation for products and support, such as 3Com, Adaptec, Inc., Digital Equipment Corp., Linksys, Xircom (portables), IBM, or Artisoft.

Installing a network card

Before you install a network card, read your computer's documentation. Become familiar with the installation directions for your network card, as well.

When you install a NIC, you must go through two steps. First, you physically install the card to the computer, and second, you install software that runs the network card. When you install that software, you also install and configure other networking software. I tell you more about the other networking software in Chapter 4.

If you're installing a network card to a portable computer, you do not remove the case from the computer. Portable computers have a door or slot for network cards that you can reach from the outside. Check your computer's documentation for more information.

Follow these steps to install a network card:

1. Make sure that you turn the computer off and unplug it before opening the case. Unplug all plugs to your computer's case, including the keyboard, mouse, monitor, and so on.

2. Remove the case. You may need to remove a few screws or simply push a button or lever. Check your computer's documentation.

Chapter 2: Choosing Network Equipment

3. Inside of the computer, look for a row of slots along the back edge. Some slots may have cards in them already. You need one open slot for your network card.

4. Remove the screw that secures the cover for the slot to the frame (it's a metal strip that keeps dust out when there's no card). Keep the screw (and the strip, too, just in case you have to remove the network card in the future and you need the strip to cover up the slot again).

5. The back of the card is the end into which you can plug a cable. This end must point toward the outside of the computer, through the slot. Holding the card only along the edges, carefully position it over the slot and gently push it straight down. When you're sure the card is correctly in place, seat the card by firmly pushing the card down into the slot. (You may have to push fairly hard.) You'll feel it snap into place.

6. Insert the screw to hold the card in place, but be careful not to tighten the screw too tight. The screw head needs to be flush with the metal tab of the card and the tab of the card should be flush to the rail of the case.

7. Check that you didn't accidentally disconnect any wires or cables in the case. Remove all tools from the case.

Do not touch the exposed parts of the computer during the next step.

8. Plug the computer in and turn it on. Watch out for smoke or the smell of something burning. Also, make sure the computer boots. If the card isn't seated properly, the computer won't boot; you won't even get video. If you detect any of these problems, turn the computer off immediately, reseat the card, and try turning the computer on again.

9. If you turned the computer on and everything seems okay, you can continue. Turn the computer off again and unplug the power cord. Replace the case and secure it with screws, if applicable. Reinstall all cables.

The next step is to connect the cabling to your network card. Again, the computer needs to be off for this process. To be safe, you might want to unplug the power cord, too.

The cable you purchased should have the correct connector on the end — Ethernet, phone jack, or other connector. All you have to do is plug the connector into the computer slot containing the card you just inserted.

Buying and Installing a Hub

A hub receives signals from the connected computers and repeats the signals to other computers on the network. You use a hub to extend the network. You need a hub only if your network uses Ethernet and connects three or more computers together. You do not need a hub if you're using telephone line or wireless connections on your network.

If you've connected two computers together using Ethernet technology, cabling, and network cards, you can do without a hub; however, you will have a faster, more efficient connection if you use a hub.

Consider the following before buying a hub:

- The first step to using a hub is to determine the technology of the cable and network card and match that technology and speed. For example, if your network cards are 10 Mbps Ethernet, your hub must be 10 Mbps Ethernet.

- The next step is to figure out how many computers you need to connect to the network. Choose a hub with at least that number of ports. Also, plan for the near future and buy a hub with at least one or two more ports than you currently need. Buying a hub that allows your network to grow is usually less expensive than having to buy a new hub later on.

- Be sure to get a hub with a lifetime warranty. Look for other benefits like cross-shipping of replacement parts and products, technical support, and so on.

When installing the hub, keep the following in mind:

- Place the hub in a central area where it will be convenient. After plugging the network cable into the network card, you can run the cable to the hub and plug it into any open port.

- Label each cable on the hub with a number or name so you know where it leads, in case you have trouble with that computer's connection.

CHAPTER 3
CONNECTING YOUR NETWORK

IN THIS CHAPTER

- Connecting only two computers
- Connecting with traditional cabling
- Using phone lines to connect
- Using wireless connections

Now that you've chosen your network hardware, it's time to tie everything together. The following sections cover the different ways you can link your network together. You can choose from various types of cabling, depending on your budget, the network speed you want, and the ease of installation. The most affordable and common cabling types for home networking are traditional cabling (Ethernet), phone line, and wireless. You can also connect two computers together in an inexpensive, rudimentary network by using a parallel or serial cable.

Connecting Only Two Computers

Using a feature in Windows 98 called *Direct Cable Connect* (DCC), you can easily share files and folders between two computers without using network cards. The connection is slow (slower than a 1 Mbps connection), but it's also inexpensive (between $15 and $25, depending on the type of cable you buy). All you have to do is attach the cable between the two computers and set up Windows 98 to use the connection. You cannot share a printer using this method; however, you can get around this inconvenience by transferring a file from one computer (without a printer) to another computer (with a printer). Then you can print the file to your heart's content using the computer with the printer.

The two computers you are connecting must be close together — at least in the same room and perhaps even on the same desk or table. The cable imposes this limit; direct cables are generally no longer than 50 feet.

DCC cable

To connect two computers, you can use a parallel file-transfer cable (also called a high-speed direct parallel cable) or a serial cable. The parallel file transfer cable costs around $25 and connects to the parallel ports (LPT) on each computer. A serial cable connects to the serial ports on each computer and costs only about $10, but it transfers data at a slower rate than a parallel cable.

Check the documentation for your computer to find out where your parallel and serial ports are located on the back of your computer.

Installing DCC

To determine whether DCC is installed on your computer, choose Start➪Programs➪Accessories➪Communications➪Direct Cable Connection. If Direct Cable Connection isn't listed on the menu, you must install it. If it is listed on the menu, skip to the next section, "Configuring DCC and connecting DCC cable."

You must install DCC on both of the computers. Follow these steps:

1. Choose Start➪Settings➪Control Panel.
2. Double-click Add/Remove Programs. The Add/Remove Programs Properties dialog box appears.
3. Click the Windows Setup tab.
4. Choose Communications and then click the Details button.
5. If Dial-Up Networking is not installed, choose it as well by clicking the check box to the left of the option. Dial-Up Networking contains features required by the direct cable connection.
6. Choose Direct Cable Connection.
7. Click OK to return to the Add/Remove Program Properties dialog box.
8. Click OK again to install the feature(s). Insert the Windows CD-ROM if prompted to. Close the Control Panel when you are finished.

Configuring DCC and connecting DCC cable

Configuring the direct cable connection and connecting the cable is relatively simple, because Windows 98 supplies a wizard to help. In order to connect the two computers, you must designate one computer as the host and one as the guest. The *host* computer provides the resources (files and folders) and the *guest* uses the resources.

After you set up the host computer, you need to go through these steps again to set up the guest computer.

Chapter 3: Connecting Your Network

To set up DCC and connect your cables, follow these steps:

1. Choose Start➪Programs➪Accessories➪Communications➪Direct Cable Connection. The Direct Cable Connection Wizard dialog box appears, as shown in Figure 3-1.

Figure 3-1: The wizard guides you though setup.

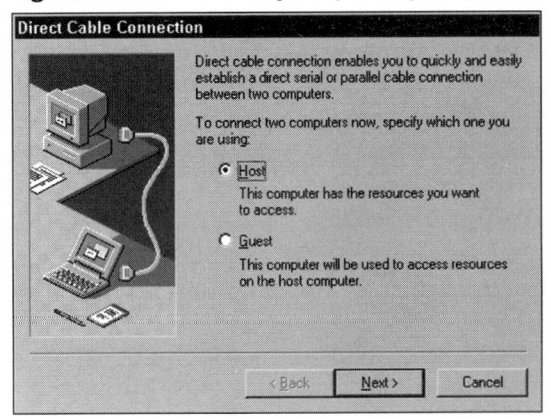

2. Choose the Host option to set up the first computer as the host computer. Click the Next button.

3. The next dialog box lists the available ports on the computer. Choose the port that corresponds with the direct cable you're using. Note that you must use the same type of port on both computers; that is, if you use a parallel port on one computer, you must use a parallel port on the other computer.

4. Plug the cable into the ports and click the Next button. The last wizard box appears, telling you that the setup was successful. If you want, you can set a password for the guest computer. Setting a password means that only users who know the password can access your computer from the other one.

After you install the host, the host computer displays a dialog box that states it is waiting for the guest computer to attach, as shown in Figure 3-2. You can now set up the guest computer. Follow the previous steps, choosing the Guest option (instead of Host) in Step 2. After you complete the guest setup, the two computers are ready to communicate with one another.

Figure 3-2: The host looks for the guest computer.

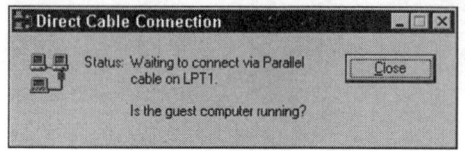

Configuring Windows 98

Before you can share files and folders, you must check the network configurations in Windows 98. Chapter 4 explains how to set up the network in detail, but here are the basic steps you need to take to set up network configurations for using DCC:

1. Locate the Network Neighborhood icon on the desktop.

2. Right-click the Network Neighborhood icon and choose Properties from the menu that appears. The Network dialog box appears.

3. In the Configuration tab, click the File and Print Sharing button. The File and Print Sharing dialog box appears.

4. Make sure that both the I Want to be Able to Give Others Access to My Files and the I Want to be Able to Allow Others to Print to My Printer check boxes are checked.

5. Click OK to close the dialog box.

6. Click the Identification tab and check your computer name and the workgroup name. Give the host and guest computers different computer names. The workgroup name must be the same on all computers in the network.

7. Go back to the Configuration tab and check to see whether a network protocol, such as TCP/IP or NetBEUI, is showing. Both computers must use the same protocol to be able to communicate over the network. When you install the adapter, a protocol for the adapter is installed at the same time.

8. Click OK to close the Network dialog box. If Windows prompts you to restart your computer, do so now.

Next, you must share the drive(s) or folder(s) you want to give others access to. For this procedure, you need to use either the Windows Explorer or My Computer features of Windows 98. For information about sharing resources, see Chapter 5.

Running the direct cable connection

Anytime you want to connect two computers with DCC, you must first start the host and then start the guest. You can use the Network Neighborhood feature of Windows 98 to view the two computers and to share files and printers.

To establish a connection between the two computers, follow these steps:

1. On the host computer, choose Start⇨Programs⇨Accessories⇨Communications⇨Direct Cable Connection. The Direct Cable Connection dialog box appears.

2. Click the Listen button. The Status dialog box appears.

3. Move to the guest computer and repeat Step 1. In the Direct Cable Connection dialog box, click the Connect button. The connection is established between the two computers.

After the two computers are connected, you can view the host from the guest anytime by clicking the View Host button in the Direct Cable Connection dialog box. When you view the host, you see the desktop as if you were sitting at that computer. You can open the Network Neighborhood and open files or folders you need to access. See Chapter 7 for more information on using the Network Neighborhood.

Connecting with Traditional Cabling

Direct cable connection is certainly inexpensive, but in certain respects, you get what you pay for. If you want to share printers, applications, games, modems, CD-ROM drives, and other peripherals in addition to sharing files and folders (and you want to do it all at higher rates of speed), you will need to invest in traditional cabling for your network.

Examining the cable

You can choose from various types of traditional cabling for your home network. The most common, efficient, and fastest cabling for home networking, however, is *twisted-pair cable*. As its name suggests, twisted-pair cable consists of two or more pairs of insulated wires twisted together and then enclosed within a plastic casing. Twisted-pair is similar to common phone wire, but twisted-pair is a higher grade of cabling that allows high-speed data to travel over it. Twisted-pair is relatively inexpensive.

Chapter 3: Connecting Your Network

Twisted-pair uses Ethernet 10BaseT standards. 10BaseT allows your network to run at 10 Mbps. Each computer in the network connects to a central hub. The maximum cable-segment length for twisted-pair is 100 meters, or 330 feet.

If you use the Ethernet 10BaseT cabling scheme, you have to buy network cards that accept Ethernet 10BaseT cabling. You also need to buy an Ethernet 10BaseT hub, one with jacks for twisted-pair connectors.

Twisted-pair cabling uses a specific connector known as an RJ-45 for attaching the cable to the network card and/or hub. An RJ-45 connector looks like an RJ-11 connector — the modular telephone jack you've seen around your house. But if you look closely, you'll see that an RJ-11 connector has only four to six pins, whereas an RJ-45 has eight pins.

There are categories, or levels, of twisted-pair cabling. Each level describes the performance characteristics of wiring standards. Of the levels of twisted-pair cabling, Category 3 (Cat 3) and Category 5 (Cat 5) are the most common. Cat 3 is less expensive than Cat 5, but its transfer rate isn't as fast. Use Cat 5 for your home network whenever possible.

Installing the cable

Installing cable can be as easy or as difficult as you want to make it. You can run the cable through walls like telephone wire or under the carpet to hide it. You can run the cable under the house or behind bookcases and around window frames. You may want to purchase *raceway,* a plastic casing that covers the cable and attaches it to the wall.

If you don't want to install the cable yourself, you can hire someone to do it. Check the yellow pages for telecommunications or telephone services, network consultants, or network technicians.

You must decide how and where you want to place the cables and where to locate the hub. The hub is best placed in a central location, easily reachable from the other rooms. Use your network map to sketch out your plan. See Chapter 1 for more on network maps.

When you're ready to actually lay the cable, label both ends of each cable with a number or name. For example, number the first cable as 1 on each end. That way, it is easier to find the cable at the hub when you're looking for a specific computer's cabling.

If you plan to go behind walls or under the floors of your house, use an electrician to help you pull the wire. For one thing, you want to avoid drilling through any electrical wiring. If you're not sure where the electrical wiring is, do not drill or pull cabling until you find out for sure. You can get a nasty electrical shock, cut the power to your home, or cause some other catastrophe.

Be very careful when installing network cabling in the walls of your house. Going through walls and under floors requires special equipment — snakes and fancy drill bits — and takes two people to pull the wire. You may need to go through cinder block walls or walls full of insulation. Watch that you don't drill through the studs in a framed wall.

Following are some more tips for installing your cable:

- Don't kink the cable. Kinks in the cable can cause connection problems as well as ruin the cable.
- Don't use a staple gun or staples of any type to install cabling. You can nick the cable, which ruins it.
- If you use a plastic or metal tie to hold several cables together, don't pull the ties too tightly. You might kink a cable and stop the connection.

- Don't install cabling so that it runs beside AC electrical wiring of any sort. The power can interfere with the data traveling over the network cable.

- Don't install cabling within two feet of fluorescent lighting. Fluorescent lights interfere with the network signal.

- If you must cross a power line, cross it at a right angle to get the least interference.

- Don't coil excess cabling when the cabling is in use. If, for example, you install the cable and have several feet left over, don't coil it up. Instead, lay the cable out as straight as possible. Coiling the cable can cause interference in the data transmissions.

Using Phone Lines to Connect

Using your phone lines to network your computers is an option you may want to explore. You can use the telephone cabling already in place at your home without rewiring or installing traditional Ethernet cabling. You can also use the RJ-11 modular phone jacks that are already in place in your home as a port for your computers.

Most phone line network kits include complete written instructions for both installing the hardware and software and configuring the computers on the network. You definitely need to install a phone line network card into each computer on your network (see Chapter 2 for more information about installing network cards), but the cabling itself is a snap. Simply plug one end of the telephone cable provided with the kit into the card's telephone port and plug the other end of the telephone cable into a wall phone jack. That's it. The cabling is done. You still have to install your network card driver, but you can find out how to do that in Chapter 4.

Using Wireless Connections

You really don't need to do much to "connect" a wireless network together. Not having any wires to connect goes without saying. Any wireless kit you buy will have instructions for setting up your network. You need to install the special NIC, which enables you to transmit your data via infrared or radio frequencies. You also need to install a wireless port on each computer on your network. The wireless ports allow the computers to send and receive data across your network. Depending on the type of wireless technology you use, you may need to position the computers close to one another or in a line-of-sight configuration (where, from one computer, you have an unobstructed view of the other computer). For more general information on wireless technologies, look at Chapter 2.

CHAPTER 4
SETTING UP THE COMPUTERS

IN THIS CHAPTER

- Installing the NIC software
- Choosing the network client
- Defining protocols
- Setting services
- Identifying the computer
- Exploring access control

Connecting all your networking hardware — cables, cards, and so on — is only half the job in setting up a home computer network. In order to get all your computers to actually talk to one another, you also have to install and set up networking software on your computers. In Windows 98, this process involves four different kinds of networking software: *client software, adapter software, service software,* and *protocol software.* Finally, you must also set your computer's identification before you can get down to the business of networking.

Installing and Configuring the Network Interface Card Software

In Windows 98 networking, an *adapter* refers to a piece of software (known as a software *driver*) that enables your computer to work together with the network interface card you installed. Windows 98 does come with a number of software drivers for NICs, listed by manufacturer and network card name, but often these drivers are not the most recent versions. The drivers contained on the floppy disks or CD-ROM that came with your network card tend to be more recent, so using them may make sense.

If at all possible, install the latest version of a NIC driver to ensure that the card works efficiently with Windows 98; you can usually download the most recent driver from a NIC manufacturer's Web site. Almost all manufacturers now include a Web address as part of their product documentation.

The adapter driver you install on Windows 98 must match up with the actual physical card you installed on your computer. See Chapter 2 for more information about installing an NIC.

Installing the NIC software

During the past few years, NIC manufacturers and Microsoft have both tried to make the bothersome task of installing NIC software easier. Newer network cards are often presented to the public as Plug and Play cards, implying that all you have to do is plug them in and your operating system (Windows 98, for example) immediately begins to "play" them without you having to change any settings. If you've installed a Plug and Play network card and you're willing to use the card's driver that came with Windows 98, installing the software ought to go pretty easily.

The first time you start up your computer after plugging in your Plug and Play network card, Windows 98 detects the card, matches it with the appropriate driver, and guides you through the installation process. Here's what you can expect:

1. The NIC software Installation Wizard appears.

2. Click Next. Windows asks if you want to locate the NIC manually or if you want Windows to do it automatically.

3. Choose to let Windows detect your NIC automatically and click Next. If Windows prompts you to insert your Windows Setup CD, do so.

4. Windows locates the NIC and installs the drivers automatically. Click Finish when Windows displays the Installation Completed Successfully dialog box.

If Windows 98 didn't automatically detect the network card driver when you turned your computer on (Plug and Play is still far from perfect, unfortunately) or you plan to install a newer version of the driver (either downloaded from the Internet or included as part of your network card package), you can add the driver yourself by following these steps:

Tip

If you download a driver for your NIC from the Internet, copy the driver to a floppy disk so you can easily install it during the steps that follow.

1. Choose Start➪Settings➪Control Panel. The Control Panel appears.

2. Double-click the Network icon to open the Network dialog box, as shown in Figure 4-1. Your Network dialog box may not look exactly like the one in the figure. Depending on your installation, one or more components may be listed.

3. In the Network dialog box, click the Add button. The Select Network Component Type dialog box appears.

4. Choose Adapter and click the Add button. The Select Network Adapters dialog box appears, as shown in Figure 4-2.

Figure 4-1: Use the Network dialog box for configuring networking software.

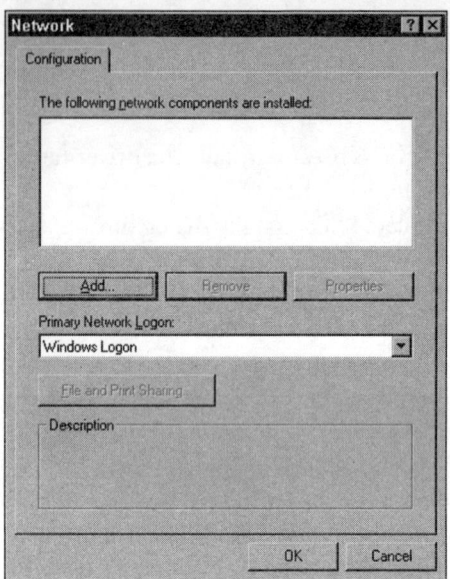

5. In the Select Network Adapters dialog box, do one of the following:

If the Plug and Play feature of your card simply wasn't cooperative and you still want to use the driver for your card that came with Windows 98, choose the name of the manufacturer of your network card in the Manufacturers list in the left window and the type of adapter in the Network Adapters list in the right window. Click OK. Windows 98 installs its version of the driver for you.

If you want to use a newer version of the driver that you have on disk, simply insert the disk containing the driver in the disk drive and click the Have Disk button. Choose the appropriate drive and click OK. Windows 98 installs your version of the driver for you.

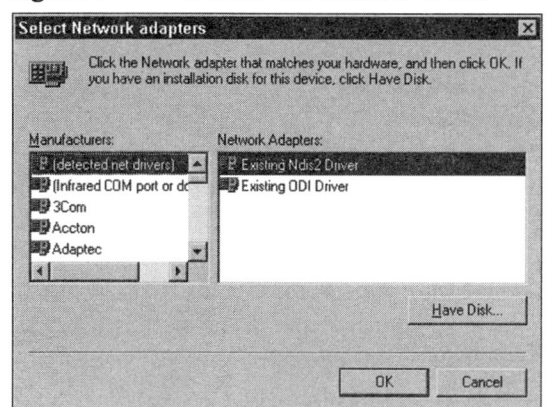

Figure 4-2: Choose the manufacturer of the card.

When Windows 98 finishes installing the network adapter, it lists the new adapter in the Network dialog box. Luckily for you, while Windows 98 was installing your adapter, it also installed a client software program (known as Client for Microsoft Networks) as well as TCP/IP as your default protocol program (*TCP/IP* is short for Transmission Control Protocol/Internet Protocol). If you'd rather use a different protocol program, you can remove TCP/IP by selecting it in the components list of the Network dialog box and clicking the Remove button. For more information on your options involving networking protocols, see the "Network Protocols" section later in this chapter.

Don't close the Network dialog box yet, because you still need it to make a few more settings changes. If you close the Network dialog box now, Windows 98 asks you to restart your computer. Save yourself the trouble of having to start and restart your computer over and over again by changing all of your settings first and then closing the Network dialog box.

Configuring the NIC software

Configuring your NIC software involves setting up a kind of pathway between the network card and your computer's processor. This setup wouldn't be a problem if there were countless pathways available for you to use, but, unfortunately, most computers have only 16 such pathways (known technically as *IRQs,* short for Interrupt Requests). What's worse, many of the IRQs are reserved for specific pieces of hardware attached to your computer, such as printers, modems, floppy disk drives, internal clocks, sound cards, keyboards, and the like, which means you can't use those IRQs for your network card. If you have a network card assigned to the same IRQ as another piece of hardware, you're going to end up with a *hardware conflict,* another way of saying that either your computer won't run or one or more of your peripherals won't work.

The Plug and Play feature of Windows 98 is supposed to automatically assign an IRQ number to your network card that doesn't conflict with other devices in your computer. That sounds like a good fix to the problem, but it tends to work only 50 percent of the time. If you are part of the lucky 50 percent, you can skip the next section. If it's not your lucky day, read on.

If you need to change the IRQ number of your network card, you can do so in the System Properties dialog box. Be very careful, however; changing settings can cause conflicts with other cards in your system. Keep a record of the original numbers and the changes you make so that you can backtrack and start over at square one again if conflicts arise. To change IRQ settings, follow these steps:

1. Choose Start➪Settings➪Control Panel and double-click the System icon. The System Properties dialog box appears.

2. Click the Device Manager tab.

3. Click the plus (+) sign to the left of Network Adapters to display your network card.

4. Double-click on the network card. The NIC's Properties dialog box appears.

5. Choose the Resources tab.

6. Remove the check mark from the Use Automatic Settings check box if it is present.

7. Choose Interrupt Request and then click the Change Settings button.

8. In the resulting dialog box, enter the new IRQ number. The most likely number for your purposes is one between 9 and 13.

9. Click OK, and then click OK twice more to get back to the Control Panel. Windows 98 prompts you to restart your computer. Do so.

Windows 98's Built-In Client Software

The *network client* is the software that enables your computer to become a member of a network. Microsoft supplies client software you can use for a Windows 98 peer-to-peer network called Client for Microsoft Networks. It's automatically installed and configured when you install your network interface card adapter software. Nice touch, right?

Network Protocols

Protocols are software programs which define the ways computers in general can transmit and receive data. In computer networks, protocols also lay down the ground rules for how computers on the network talk with one another. Windows 98 comes with three different network protocols to choose from. They are:

- **NetBEUI:** The Microsoft protocol designed to work with Windows 98. NetBEUI (short for Network Basic Input Output System Extended User Interface) is perfect for small peer-to-peer networks — it's easy to set up, it provides good performance, and it's a fast protocol. NetBEUI uses very little memory. If you're setting up your first network and you want an easy job of it, use NetBEUI as your networking protocol.

- **TCP/IP:** The protocol of the Internet, it can also be used on your home network. TCP/IP is versatile, is fast, and provides a wide variety of options for configuration. Because TCP/IP is difficult to configure, however, you probably don't want to use it in your home network if you're just learning about protocols and networking.

- **IPX/SPX:** A protocol frequently used with Novell NetWare networks, although you can also use it with Microsoft networks. Unless you have a specific reason for using IPX/SPX (short for Internet Package Exchange/Sequenced Package Exchange) — such as integration with a NetWare network — stick with NetBEUI. IPX/SPX doesn't offer as much for Microsoft networks as the NetBEUI or TCP/IP protocols do.

Installing a protocol

Installing protocols is actually a piece of cake. You may remember that Windows 98 even installs TCP/IP for you as the default protocol. The default TCP/IP is something of a mixed blessing, however. Having TCP/IP as your default protocol requires you to assign a unique address (known as an *IP address*) to each computer on your network. I show you how to do that in the "Configuring TCP/IP" section later in this chapter.

Because you must use the same protocol for all computers on the network, you must install the same protocol on each computer. To do so, complete the following steps for each computer:

1. Open the Network dialog box by choosing Start➪Settings➪Control Panel and then double-clicking the Network icon. The Network dialog box appears.

2. In the Network dialog box, click the Add button. The Select Network Component Type dialog box appears.

3. Choose Protocol in the network component list.

4. Click the Add button. The Select Network Protocol dialog box appears.

5. In the Manufacturers list, choose Microsoft.

6. Choose a protocol from the list, as shown in Figure 4-3.

7. Click OK to add the protocol. Windows 98 returns to the Network dialog box when it is done. Restart the computer when prompted.

Figure 4-3: Installing the NetBEUI protocol.

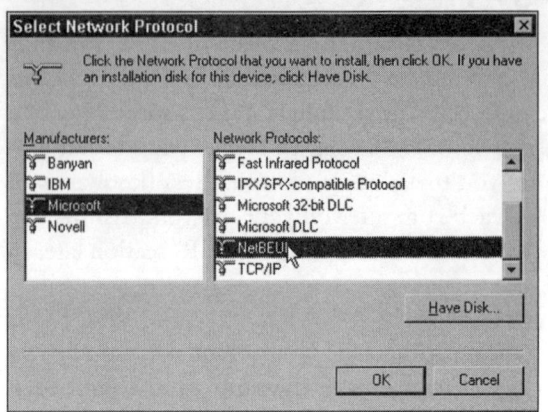

Configuring TCP/IP

Because TCP/IP uses a special system of binary numbers for identifying computers on the network, you must configure each computer with a unique IP address using this numbering system in order for TCP/IP to work.

If you're a Windows 98 user, you're in luck: Windows 98 includes LinkLocal, a method of assigning unique IP addresses that makes assigning IP addresses a whole lot easier. As you configure each computer on the network, LinkLocal keeps track of the addresses used and ensures that each computer receives a unique address. **Note:** Windows 95 does not include LinkLocal.

To enable LinkLocal, follow these steps:

1. Choose Start➪Settings➪Control Panel. The Control Panel window appears.

2. Double-click the Network icon. The Network dialog box appears.

3. Choose the TCP/IP Ethernet adapter and click the Properties button. The TCP/IP Properties dialog box appears, as shown in Figure 4-4.

4. In the IP Address tab of the TCP/IP Properties dialog box, select the Obtain an IP Address Automatically option, if it is not already selected.

5. Click OK to close the TCP/IP Properties dialog box.

6. Click OK again to close the Network dialog box. Windows 98 prompts you to restart the computer. Go ahead and do so. When you start the computer again, it automatically assigns itself an IP address.

Figure 4-4: Configure TCP/IP.

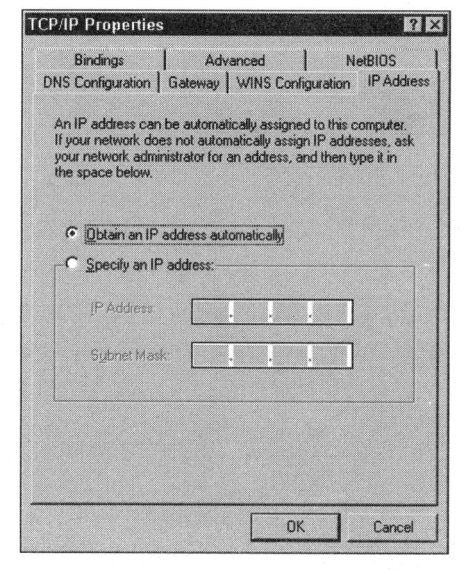

You must repeat these steps with each computer on the network to complete the process. When you're finished, your network is up and running using the TCP/IP protocol.

Setting Services

Part of the whole rationale for having a computer network is based on your desire to share certain resources (such as files, folders, and printers) over the network. You have to make your wishes clear to Windows 98, however, by first laying down some ground rules. You do so by defining your *network services*. For example, you can choose to share your files but not your printer or your printer but not your files. You lay down the ground rules by adding the network services you want in the Network dialog box and then specifying your options. Follow these steps:

1. Open the Network dialog box by choosing Start➪Settings➪Control Panel and double-clicking the Network icon. The Network dialog box appears.

2. In the Network dialog box, click the Add button. The Select Network Component Type dialog box appears.

3. Choose Service.

4. Click the Add button. The Select Network Service dialog box appears.

5. Choose Microsoft from the manufacturers listed in the left window and File and Printer Sharing for Microsoft Networks from the network services listed in the right window.

6. Click OK. Windows 98 adds the service to the network components window.

7. If you want to share your files but not your printer or your printer but not your files, open the Network dialog box again and click the File and Print Sharing button. The File and Print Sharing dialog box appears, as shown in Figure 4-5.

8. Click the appropriate check box to clear it if you want to pick and choose between sharing your files or your printer with others on the network. Then click OK.

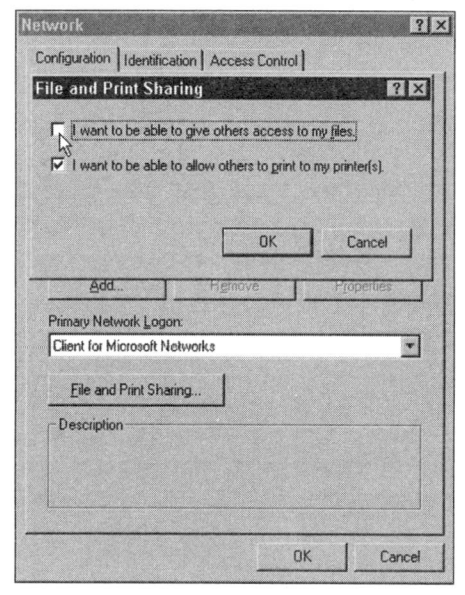

Figure 4-5: Limit file and printer sharing.

Identifying the Computer

Even if you're not bothering with TCP/IP and its system of IP addresses, you still must identify your computer to the network. Otherwise, computers on the network won't be able to find each other. Windows 98 makes it easy for you by letting you identify each computer in the Computer Identification tab of the Network dialog box.

To identify the computer to the network, follow these steps:

1. Open the Network dialog box by choosing Start ⇨ Settings ⇨ Control Panel and double-clicking the Network icon. The Network dialog box appears.

2. Choose the Identification tab.

3. In the Computer Name text box, enter a unique name for the computer. It can be the name of a family member, the name of a famous artist, or even the name of a constellation. Just be sure that the name makes sense to all individuals using the network.

4. In the Workgroup text box, enter the name of your workgroup. You can simply use your family's last name. The workgroup name must be the same on all computers on the network.

5. If you want, you can enter a brief description of the computer (brand name, type of processor, built-in memory, and so on), as shown in Figure 4-6.

6. Choose OK. When Windows 98 prompts you to restart your computer, click Yes to restart.

You need to repeat all of the preceding steps with each computer on the network. If you add one kind of client, protocol, and service software to a computer, you must add the same kind to all computers. Also be sure that you install the adapter software designed to work with your network interface card. Finally, don't forget that although each computer has its own unique computer name, you have to have a common workgroup name on all computers for them to be able to talk to one another across the network.

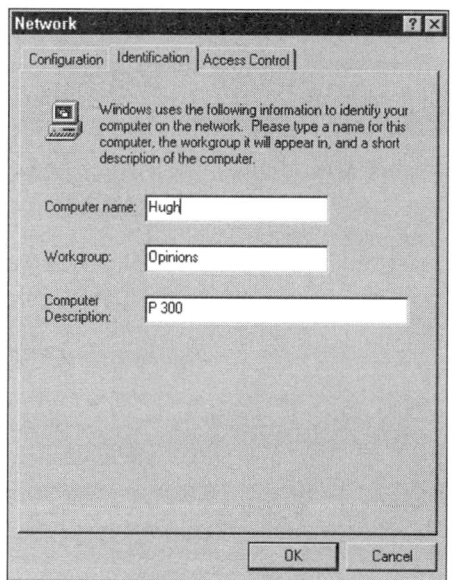

Figure 4-6: Identify the computer to the network.

Exploring Access Control

The Access Control tab of the Network dialog box offers two options for controlling the access to shared resources: Share-level and User-level. Use Share-level access for a peer-to-peer network. User-level works best with a client/server network, such as Windows NT Server or Novell NetWare. The default option is Share-level, so you don't have to make any changes to this tab.

Share-level access control lets you supply a password for each shared resource. If you want to be particular about who gets to share a folder or printer, you can use Access Control to assign a password to that resource. Only people who know the password may then access that resource. Of course, you don't have to use passwords for sharing resources, but it's nice to know that you have the capability to do so if you want to.

User-level access control works by assigning specific users (or groups of users) access to resources on the computer. Because of their larger size, client/server networks often use groups for authentication and permissions purposes. User-level access works better in that kind of environment, but isn't normally something you need to worry about on a smaller home network.

CHAPTER 5
SHARING FOLDERS, DRIVES, FILES, AND INTERNET ACCESS

IN THIS CHAPTER

- Understanding limits and permissions
- Sharing a folder
- Sharing a drive
- Sharing a file
- Sharing Internet access

One major reason you connect your computer to a network is so that you can share resources with others. Resources refer to files, folders, drives, printers, CD-ROM drives, Iomega Zip or Jaz drives (handy hardware for backing up a large number of files), and so on. You probably want to share most of your computer resources with your spouse and children, or you and your spouse may want to share files containing letters, household accounting information, or genealogy data. Older children in your home may want to share their homework files with you so that you can review them before they print them out. Of course, you likely want to share printers, CD-ROM drives, and other hardware as well.

Understanding Sharing and Access Limits

You may not want to share everything on your computer, however. Networks are designed so that you can also *limit* the access to shared resources in case you have confidential information to protect or equipment that's too expensive for children to use.

Access types

Windows 98 lets you limit the access to any file, folder, drive, or other resource by assigning them an *access type*. Following are the access types from which you can choose:

- **Read-only.** Allows others either to open and view folders or to open, view, and copy files; however, read-only access doesn't allow others to change a file or delete anything.

- **Full.** Lets anyone open, change, add, or remove files and folders.

- **Depends on Password.** You can set a password on any resource so that only the people who know the password have access to that resource. You can give your spouse password access, for example, but limit your children from access to a specific resource. Using password limits, you can also choose read-only or full access.

Share designation

Windows 98 gives you another option for sharing resources. In addition to setting access limits to individual files or folders, you can also set up entire sections of your computer for a kind of blanket sharing. You might, for example, share an entire drive on your hard disk.

A Windows 98 computer has a lot of folders, and you don't need to share them all by any means. See the "Identifying folders to share" section later in this chapter for more information.

Sharing Folders, Drives, and Files

In a perfect world, sharing your entire hard disk would be the simplest way to set up a share. The world is far from perfect, however, and if you're concerned that sharing your entire hard disk drive is asking for trouble, you may want to take the time to choose specific folders for sharing. As always, plan ahead. For your network to work properly, you have to have a clear idea of which folders you want to share.

Before you can share any resource on the network, you must first install the networking software and hardware. When installing the networking software, you must enable file and print sharing services. See Chapter 4 for more information.

Identifying folders to share

By now you know that you share your folders to provide documents and files to others on the network. You may not know that you don't need to (and shouldn't) share many of your folders at all.

Following are just a few of the folders not to share:

- You don't need to share your Windows folder. The Windows folder holds all the files that make Windows work, including fonts, configuration files, programming files, help files, and so on. Changes to this folder can cause real problems (as in, Windows won't be able to run on your computer).

- You may not want to share your Program Files folder. Each Program Files folder contains a number of software application folders, including folders for Internet Explorer, Microsoft Office, Outlook, NetMeeting, and so on. Each application folder contains the files that make a specific program run. More than likely, the other network computers contain these applications and, therefore, don't need to share yours. Moreover, sharing these folders invites the kind of accidental or deliberate changes that may keep these programs from running.

- Don't share any folders that contain *device drivers*. (Device drivers are the software programs that run your computer hardware and peripherals — your CD-ROM drive, network card, tape backup, and so on). Because these folders contain data specific to your computer, no one else needs them. If someone were to accidentally delete a device driver folder, your system could stop functioning properly.

Following are the folders you do want to share:

- Share a specific program file folder. Say you use Quicken for your personal accounting program. If you store your account data in the Quicken folder (C:\Program Files\QuickenW\My Data, for example), you may want to share the Quicken folder so that your spouse can access the data too.

- You can share folders that contain data that others may want or need (your My Documents folder, for example, or other folders you've created to contain documents).

- You can share application folders that others can copy, such as the WinZip folder (WinZip is a file compression program). If your spouse reformats a drive and wants to copy your WinZip program to install to the new drive, copying it from your hard drive over the network is the quickest and easiest method.

Designating a shared folder

In order to share folders, you first need a convenient way of locating the folders on your computer. Both the Windows Explorer and My Computer features of Windows 98 allow you to conveniently locate folders by letting you navigate quickly through your various directories until you find the folder you want. After you locate the folder using Windows Explorer or My Computer, you can then designate any folder as shared.

To designate a folder as shared, follow these steps (I use the My Computer feature in this example):

1. Double-click the My Computer icon on your desktop. The My Computer window appears. Navigate down through the directories until you find the folder you want.

2. Select the folder, as shown in Figure 5-1.

3. Right-click the selected folder and choose Sharing from the menu that appears. The folder's Properties dialog box appears with the Sharing tab displayed.

4. In the Sharing tab, choose the Shared As option, as shown in Figure 5-2. The share name for your folder is displayed in the Share Name text box. (The *share name* is the name others on the network see when they want to access the folder over the network.) The share name is exactly the same as the original name of the folder. If you want to change the folder name, simply delete the text in the Share Name text box and type a new name.

Putting an ampersand (&) in front of the folder's name forces the folder to display at the top of the folder list in Windows Explorer and My Computer.

5. If you want, you can enter text in the Comment text box of the Sharing dialog box. Comments can describe the documents within a folder, for example.

Figure 5-1: Select the folder to be shared.

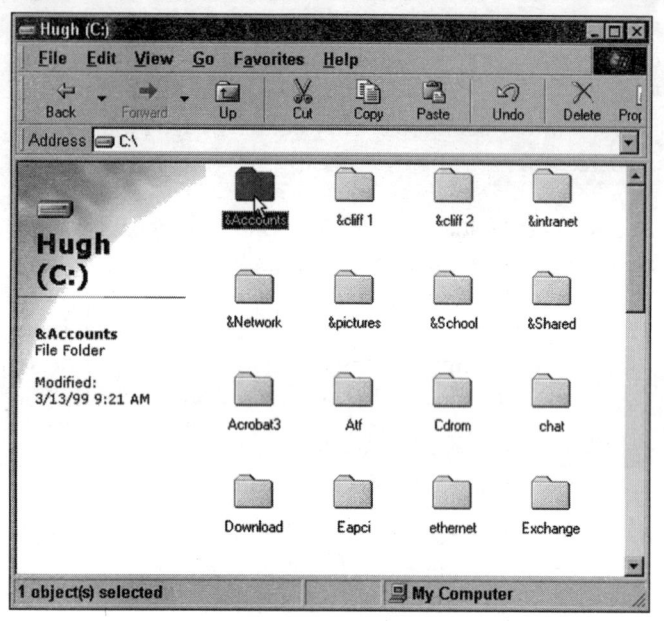

6. In Access Type, choose one of the following access types:

Read-only. You can apply the limit with or without a password. If you want to add a password, enter it in the Read-Only Password text box.

Full. If you want to assign a password to a folder with full access, enter that word in the Full Access Password text box.

Depends on Password. Choose this option if you want to apply passwords to both a read-only and a full access. Enter the passwords in the appropriate text box in the Passwords section.

Chapter 5: Sharing Folders, Drives, Files, and Internet Access

7. Click OK to accept the changes and close the dialog box.

When you share a folder (or a drive or a file) from your computer, an outstretched hand icon appears on that object in both the Windows Explorer and My Computer windows.

Figure 5-2: Accept the default or enter a new name.

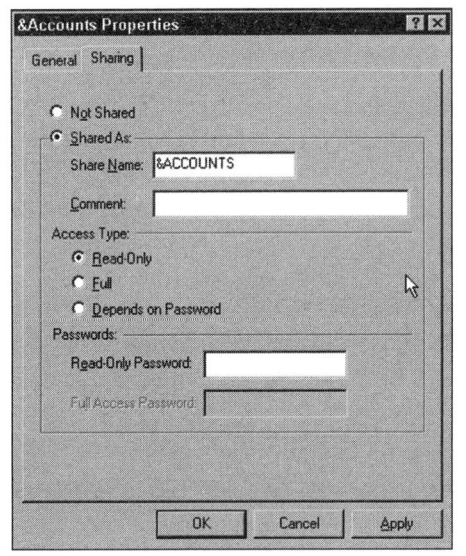

> Shared folders from other computers on the network do not display the outstretched hand by the folder or drive icon. Only your own folders display that shared symbol.

Designating a shared drive

Sharing a drive may not be the safest way to share resources over the network, but it's certainly the easiest. After installing the appropriate software and hardware, you simply designate drives as shared the same way you would designate folders as shared: locate the drive by using either the Windows Explorer or the My Computer features of Windows 98, right-click the drive to access the Properties dialog box, and choose the Shared As option in the Sharing tab. You have the same access options that you have with folders, and when you're done, the same little outstretched hand icon appears on your drive icon. Everyone on your network now has access to everything on the shared drive.

Designating a file as shared

Sharing files using the networking features of Windows 98 is simple: When you share a folder or a drive, all files in that folder or drive are automatically shared. However, no easy way exists to set up a situation so that only certain files within a folder or drive can be shared.

If you want to keep a file within a shared folder yet still control access to the file, you may be able to do so by using the built-in password option of the program you use to create the file, but this option is possible only with certain programs. Microsoft Word, for example, allows you to save a file as password-protected, meaning that an individual would need to know a password in order to open or change a file.

If this method seems like too much trouble or your software program doesn't offer a built-in password feature, simply store the files you want to keep private in a separate folder that doesn't offer any share access at all. When it comes to privacy issues, the best policy is always to refrain from sharing anything you don't want others to see.

Chapter 5: Sharing Folders, Drives, Files, and Internet Access

Sharing Internet Access

Many people use their home computers for Internet access. Surfing the Web, e-mailing family and friends, and joining discussion groups can provide every member of the family with hours of fun and learning. You can set up your Windows 98 network so that everyone connected can access the Internet through one user account quickly and easily.

Tip: If you use Windows 98 Second Edition, you can purchase the Microsoft "step-up" CD for around $20. This CD offers several programs you can use with Windows, including an Internet-sharing application.

The basics of using a modem and setting up an Internet account with an Internet Service Provider (or ISP) are the same whether you are on a computer network or not. If you need help with the basics, check out CliffsNotes *Getting on the Internet*. If you are already set up for the Internet and want to find out how you can share Internet access over your network, read on.

Using third-party applications

A *modem* (the piece of hardware that uses your phone line to connect to the Internet) is not usually set up to allow sharing over a computer network. However, if you use your modem in combination with some additional software (known as *third-party applications,* because they are provided neither by the manufacturer of your computer nor by the modem's manufacturer), you can surf the Net and send and receive e-mail at the same time others on the network use the Internet connection. Various programs exist that allow you to turn one phone line into multiple Internet connections.

> **Warning:** Many ISPs do not allow you to share one Internet account in this manner. Check to see if yours does.

Most of these software applications require you to use TCP/IP as your network protocol. See Chapter 4 for more information about network protocols.

You install the modem-sharing software to a host machine first; this is the computer that's attached directly to the modem. Then you install the software to the other computers, or guests. The host computer runs the service and is prepared to dial up the Internet account when a guest requests the service.

Software options

Many products exist that enable you to share a connection to the Internet. Following are a few of those programs:

- **WinGate** (Obik New Zealand Ltd.): Lets you simultaneously connect multiple users to the Internet using one Internet account and one modem. Installation and configuration are easy. Three versions of the program exist: WinGate Standard, WinGate Home, and WinGate Pro. Each version offers different features. Prices are based on the number of users and the version. For example, WinGate Home sells for around $40 for three users and $70 for six users. WinGate Standard sells for around $80 for three users and $140 for six users. See www.wingate.com for more information.

- **Rideway** (ITServ): Lets you assign each computer on the network an internal IP address. The IP address means you have to use the TCP/IP protocol on your network. If you plan to use TCP/IP anyway, Rideway might be the choice for you. It costs about $30 to set up two PCs to share an Internet account.

- **WinProxy** (Ositis Internet Sharing Software): Easy and inexpensive to use. Install the host software to a computer attached to the modem, and other computers on the network can get e-mail, join newsgroups, download files, and otherwise use the Internet connection through one machine. The WinProxy Lite version, which enables three connections at a time, costs less than $70.

CHAPTER 6
GETTING ON (AND AROUND) THE NETWORK

IN THIS CHAPTER

- Logging on and off
- Using network paths to find folders and files
- Mapping drives
- Finding computers on the network

After you have set up your various files, folders, and drives for sharing, you still have to find out how to use the networking capabilities of Windows 98 to your best advantage. Working on the network is a bit different than working on a non-networked computer. You need to understand how to access the network and how to best get to the computers and files you need. Windows 98 offers several shortcuts for finding the files and folders you need on the network, including network paths, mapped drives, and the Find Computer feature.

Logging On and Off

When you log on to a Windows 98 non-networked computer, you enter your Windows username and password. Logging on to Windows 98 identifies you to the operating system, which can then display your personal settings for your programs, your passwords to the Internet, and so on. Logging on allows multiple users to access one computer and keep their individual preferences and desktop settings.

Logging on to the network is similar. When you log on to the network by entering your username and password, Windows 98 immediately identifies you as a valid member of the network group and enables you to access files, folders, printers, and other resources made available to you. For more information on access privileges, see Chapter 5.

Looking at usernames

Your *username* is the name by which you're known to the network. You can use your first name or a nickname, for example. You can use any combination of letters (upper or lower case) and numbers. If you want, you can even include spaces within a name, so you can use your first and last name the way you're used to writing it (Sue Plumley, for example.) Passwords are case sensitive; you must use the same upper- and/or lowercase letters each time you enter the password.

Considering passwords

A *password* is normally an identifier for an authorized user to gain access to the network. You can use passwords for security purposes on a client/server network, but on a peer-to-peer Windows 98 network, the password doesn't really keep anyone from accessing the network. On a peer-to-peer network, anyone can log onto any computer at any time. For example, one of your teenagers' friends can turn on a networked computer and enter his or her name and any password he or she chooses. If you have not been strict about setting access types, that person can then open the Network Neighborhood and access the shared folders and drives on your computer. If that prospect scares you, you may consider toughening up your access limits by relying more on share passwords. For more information on using passwords, see Chapter 5.

Logging off of the network

You can log off the network if you have two or more people sharing your computer and you want to give someone else time on the network. You log off so that the other person can access his or her network resources. If you don't share your computer with someone else, you don't need to log off in a peer-to-peer situation. You can stay logged in all day if you like.

Remember: When you shut down your computer, you're automatically logged off and your resources are no longer available.

To log off of the network, follow these steps:

1. Save all open files and close all programs. You must do this before logging off so that you don't lose any data.

2. Choose Start➪Log Off ...(your username). Windows 98 displays the Log Off Windows dialog box, which asks if you're sure you want to log off.

3. Click Yes to log off. (If you change your mind, click No to cancel the dialog box and return to the desktop).

4. After you click Yes, Windows 98 displays a new Enter Network Password dialog box. The new user should enter a username and password to log back on to the network.

Using Network Paths to Find Folders and Files

A *pathname* defines the route through the various directories and folders your computer must take to reach a folder or file. If you know the pathname for a certain file or folder, you can use that information to quickly jump to that file or folder.

Chapter 6: Getting on (And around) the Network

Determining the pathname of a file or folder on your own computer isn't that difficult. You simply start the pathname with the appropriate drive and then list the folders with the outermost folder first. For example, if you stored your Pictures folder within your My Documents folder on your C drive, then the pathname would be C:\My Documents\Pictures. Notice that the single backslashes after the name of the C drive and after the name of each folder are part of the pathname.

When you need to determine a pathname for a drive found on a computer somewhere else on the network, you must first list the computer and then the shared folders. Such a *network path* always begins with two backslashes (\\) to indicate that the drive is on another computer on the network. For example, if you want to write a path from your computer to the folder C:\Netshares\Documents\Letters\Utilities on another computer you've named Sue, you type the following: \\Sue\Netshares\Documents\Letters\Utilities.

If you are good at remembering pathnames, you can use them to jump immediately to the file or folder you want on your network. The Windows Explorer, My Computer, and Network Neighborhood windows all have an address bar near the top where you can enter the pathname, press Enter, and end up where you wanted to go.

If you want, you can also get where you want to go on your computer network by using the Run dialog box as shown in Figure 6-1. Choose Start➪Run, type in the path name in the text box, and press Enter, and Windows 98 will take you immediately to the file or folder you want. For all this to work without a hitch, however, the other computer must be turned on, the folder you want must be a shared folder, and you have to have permission to access the folder.

Figure 6-1: Use a path to access another computer.

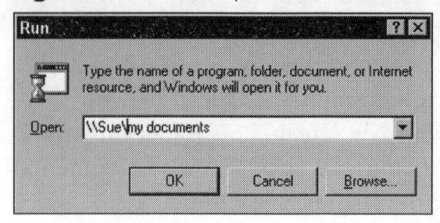

Figure 6-2 shows the results of entering the path in the Run dialog box. The My Documents folder on Sue's computer opens for your use.

Figure 6-2: Quickly access a folder if you know the path.

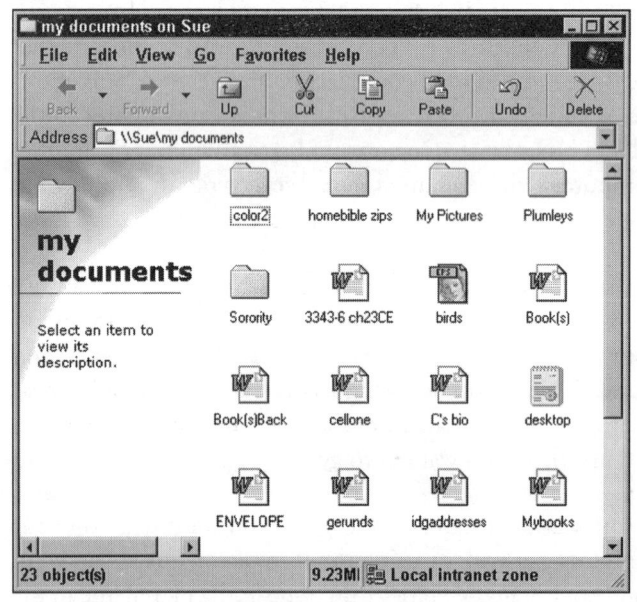

Mapping Drives

If you connect to a specific drive and folder on one of your networked computers every day (or even several times a day), you may find yourself wishing for a shortcut. One option

Chapter 6: Getting on (And around) the Network

that may work for you involves *mapping drives,* where you assign a new drive letter (such as J, K, L, M, N or any other letter not currently in use) to the drive you're interested in.

Unfortunately, you can only map to one folder level. For example, you cannot map to \\Sue\My Documents\Pictures; you can only map to \\Sue\My Documents. Every little bit helps, however, and you'll find that mapping drives can make your networking life easier.

To map a drive, follow these steps:

1. On the Windows desktop, right-click the My Computer icon. A quick menu appears.

2. Choose Map Network Drive. The Map Network Drive dialog box appears, as shown in Figure 6-3.

Figure 6-3: Use the Map Network Drive dialog box to map a drive.

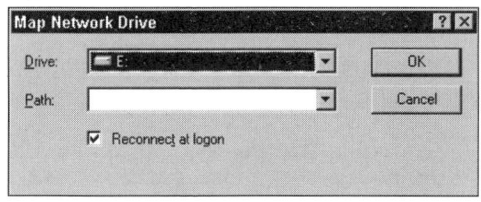

3. In the Drive drop-down list box, choose a drive letter to represent the folder you're going to map. Only available drive letters appear; you won't see drive letters already used for other drives (CD-ROM or hard drives, for example).

4. In the Path text box, enter the network path to the folder.

5. Click the Reconnect at Logon check box if you want the mapped drive to connect automatically when you log on to the network.

6. Click OK. The mapped drive is now stored with the other drives in the My Computer window.

If the folder to which you are mapping a drive has an assigned password, the Enter Network Password dialog box appears. The first time you connect to the drive, you can save the password in your password list (PWL file) by choosing the Save This Password in Your Password List option. From then on, Windows 98 will remember the password and enter it for you when you log on.

Accessing a mapped drive

Accessing a mapped drive is as easy as mapping it in the first place. To access a folder on a mapped drive, follow these steps:

1. On the desktop, double-click My Computer. The My Computer window appears, as shown in Figure 6-4.

2. Double-click the mapped drive to display the contents of the mapped folder.

3. Open any file by double-clicking the appropriate file icon.

Disconnecting a mapped drive

If you find that you are no longer using a mapped drive with any real frequency, you can easily delete it from your drives listing. In Windows 98 terminology, this is known as *disconnecting* a mapped drive.

To disconnect a mapped drive, follow these steps:

1. Right-click the My Computer icon on your desktop.

Chapter 6: Getting on (And around) the Network

2. Choose Disconnect Network Drive from the menu that appears. The Disconnect Network Drive dialog box appears.

3. In the list of drives, choose the drive you want to delete.

4. Click OK to disconnect the network connection.

Figure 6-4: Access the mapped drive.

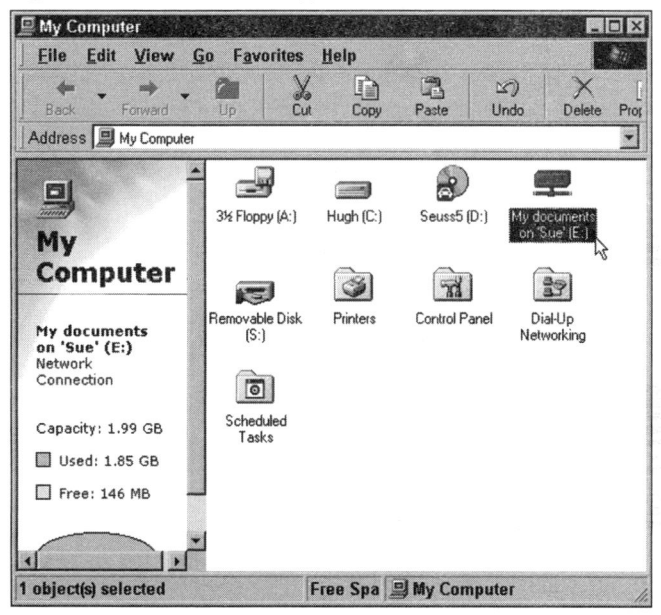

Applying Quick Logon

As long as you always check the Reconnect at Logon check box in the Map Network Drive dialog box, your computer reconnects to any drives you have mapped whenever you log on to the network.

Reconnecting network drives takes time, however, and the more mapped drives you have, the longer it takes. Moreover, if a computer you're trying to connect to isn't turned on,

Windows notifies you that it cannot map the drive and offers the option of reconnecting to the networked computer the next time you log on. Getting your computer started takes even longer when this complication happens.

You do have an option, however, of logging on more quickly. A *quick logon* ignores any network drive connections you may have set so that you can get on the network and start working immediately. Don't worry. You can restore these connections easily when you need them. All you have to do is double-click the mapped drive icon to connect the drive.

To set your computer for quick logon, follow these steps:

1. Choose Start⇨Settings⇨Control Panel.
2. Double-click the Network icon to display the Network dialog box.
3. In the Configuration tab, choose Client for Microsoft Networks from the network components list.
4. Click the Properties button. The Client for Microsoft Networks Properties dialog box appears, as shown in Figure 6-5.
5. In the Network Logon options box, choose Quick Logon.

It's best to choose Quick Logon if the other computers in your network are not always going to be on. If you choose to restore network connections and a network computer isn't turned on, your computer will search for a long time before asking you to cancel the connection.

Figure 6-5: Set quick logon.

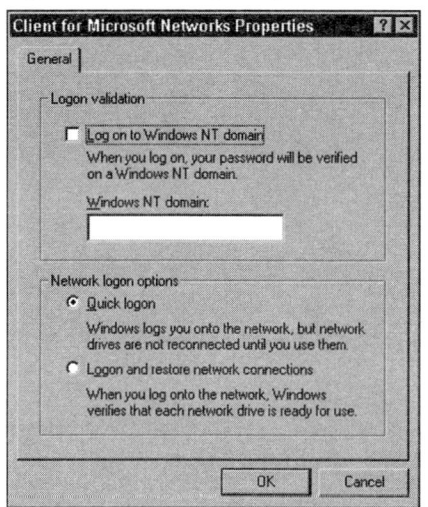

Finding Computers on the Network

You're probably familiar with the Find command in Windows 98 (that is, choosing Start➪Find and then usually choosing Files or Folders). This command is commonly used to find files and folders on your local hard drive or on CD-ROM drives. As part of the Find command, you can also find computers on the network as long as the computer is turned on, the files are shared, and you have access to them.

Finding a computer

If you know the name of a computer on the network, you can find it by using the same Find command you use to find files or folders. To find a computer, simply choose Start➪Find➪Computer. The Find dialog box appears, as shown in Figure 6-6.

Figure 6-6: Find a computer on the network.

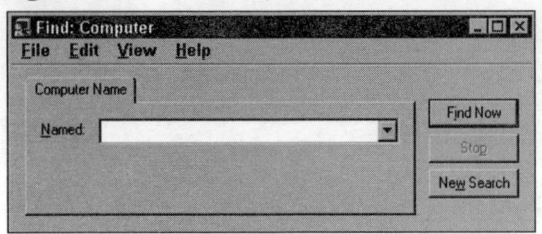

Enter the computer's name in the Named text box and click Find Now. If the computer is found, the Find Computer dialog box enlarges to display the computer's name, as shown in Figure 6-7.

Figure 6-7: Locate the computer by name.

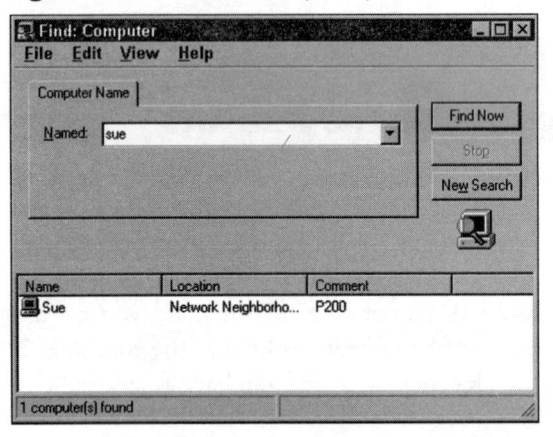

Double-click the computer's name to display all the shared resources stored on that computer. From here, depending on your access rights, you can read files, copy folders, delete files, revise a word processing file, or edit a spreadsheet. If you have full access rights to the networked computer, you can basically treat it as if it were your own computer.

Finding a networked folder

In addition to finding a networked computer with the Find Computer dialog box, you can use the same dialog box to find a specific folder on the network, as long as you know the path to the folder. You can, for example, enter \\Sue\&pictures\house and Find Computer locates the folder on the computer and displays it.

After you locate the folder, you can open it by double-clicking it in the Find Computer dialog box. Again, depending on your access rights, you can delete or rename the folder, view its properties, cut or copy it, or change the view. Simply use the menus in the Find Computer dialog box to perform any of these commands on the selected folder.

CHAPTER 7
USING THE NETWORK NEIGHBORHOOD

IN THIS CHAPTER

- Browsing the Network Neighborhood
- Working with files and folders
- Accessing resources using shortcuts

Although you can use the Windows Explorer or My Computer windows to browse the network, the Network Neighborhood for Windows 98 is built specifically for viewing and using network computers and files. You can view networked computers' files and folders as well as copy, move, rename, or delete them.

Browsing the Network Neighborhood

The Network Neighborhood is the Windows 98 mini-program designed specifically for working with networked computers, folders, and other resources. When you first open the Network Neighborhood, all connected computers appear on-screen, as shown in Figure 7-1. You don't have to enter a pathname or double-click icons to get to the network.

To open the Network Neighborhood, double-click the icon on the desktop.

To view any computer's contents, simply double-click the icon associated with that computer. All shared resources on the computer appear in the Network Neighborhood, as shown in Figure 7-2. If you like, you can change the view

Chapter 7: Using the Network Neighborhood   **79**

from large icons to small icons, list, or details by choosing the View menu and selecting the view you want.

Figure 7-1:   Use the Network Neighborhood to view network computers.

Use the following methods to navigate through the Network Neighborhood window and browse the networked computers:

- To open a folder, double-click the folder or choose File➪Open.

- To move back to the previous window, click the Back button on the toolbar.

- To go forward again to the next window, click the Forward button.

- To move back to the entire network view, choose File➪Network Neighborhood. The File menu lists the most recent computers, drives, and/or folders you browsed. You can use this list to quickly return to a location in the Network Neighborhood window.

Figure 7-2: View a computer's contents.

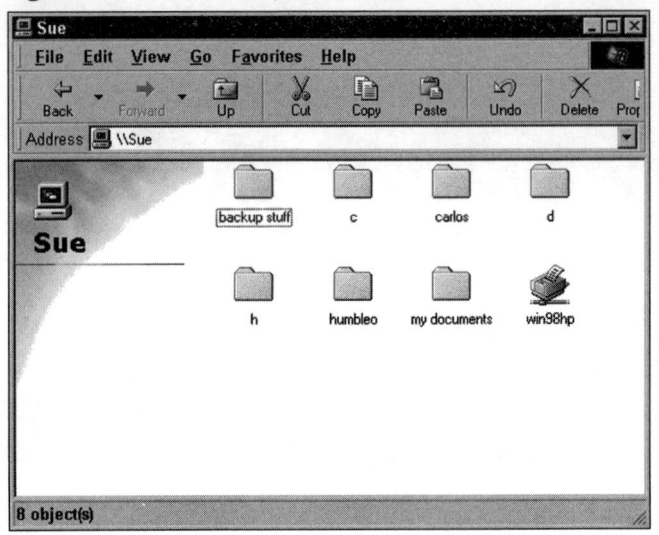

- You can use the Address bar to enter a path to a computer and folder(s). See Chapter 6 for information about network paths.

The Entire Network icon represents additional network printers and folders that are available to your computer. Double-click the icon to display additional resources.

Working with Files and Folders

In addition to making it easier to keep an eye on all aspects of your network, the Network Neighborhood includes all of the features and tools you're used to seeing in My Computer and Windows Explorer. You can rename or delete files and folders you view in the Network Neighborhood as well as create shortcuts from your desktop to the file or folder you're interested in anywhere on the network. You can cut or copy files and folders from one networked computer and paste them to another. If you want, you can also use the Find feature of Network Neighborhood to find files.

The files and folders must be shared and the networked computer with which you're working must be turned on for you to be able to work with a networked computer's files and folders. If a password is required to access the folders, you must know that password.

You should make sure you ask or at least notify the owner of the files or folders before you delete, rename, or otherwise change the files and folders on a networked computer.

Finding files

Although you can use your Find command to find a networked folder, you do have to remember the folder's pathname. Sometimes a folder's pathname will escape you. You could browse the network searching for a file, but you can also quickly locate a file on another computer by using Network Neighborhood's Find feature.

To quickly locate a file on another computer using Network Neighborhood, follow these steps:

1. Double-click the Network Neighborhood icon on your desktop. The Network Neighborhood window appears.

2. Double-click the icon of the computer you're interested in. The computer's folders are displayed in a new window.

3. Select the folder containing the file.

4. Choose File⇔Find. The Find All Files dialog box appears.

5. Enter the name of the file or a word or phrase contained within the file. See Chapter 6 for more information about the Find File dialog box.

CliffsNotes Setting Up a Windows 98 Home Network

6. Click the Find Now button. Windows locates the file in the folder, as shown in Figure 7-3.ced You can open, print, copy, or otherwise work with the file from the Find All Files dialog box.

Figure 7-3: Find a file.

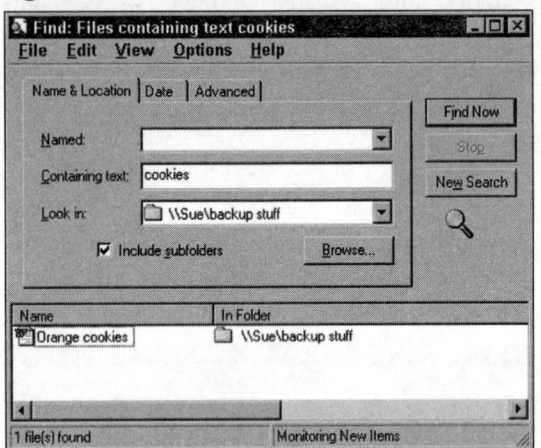

Creating a shortcut

If you often use a file or folder on another computer, you're not limited to mapping a drive to access that folder. You can also use Network Neighborhood to create a *shortcut* on your desktop. The shortcut makes accessing the folder or file quick and easy.

To create a shortcut, follow these steps:

1. Open the networked computer in the Network Neighborhood window.
2. Locate the folder or file you want to create a shortcut for.
3. Right-click the folder. Choose Create Shortcut from the pop-up menu that appears.
4. Windows displays a message that it cannot create the shortcut in the window and asks if you want the shortcut on your desktop instead. Click Yes.

5. Windows places the shortcut on your desktop.

> **Remember:** The shortcut you create doesn't indicate that it's a shortcut to a network computer. For example, the shortcut name might be "Shortcut to My Documents." You can, however, change the name of the shortcut to better identify it, such as "Sue's Documents." To change the name of a shortcut, right-click the shortcut on your desktop and choose Rename. Enter the name you want.

Creating, deleting, and renaming files and folders

Network Neighborhood offers great opportunities to put your networking house in order. When you're inside Network Neighborhood, you can create new folders, delete and rename files and folders, and do other housekeeping chores for any of your networked computers by using the same commands you used for your non-networked Windows 98 computer. Using the familiar options under the File command (File➪New➪Folder, File➪Rename, and File➪Delete), you can now range far and wide over your network and clean house to your heart's content. Simply double-click on the computer you want in the Network Neighborhood list to access the computer and then put your organizational talents to use.

Copying and moving files and folders

Another great housekeeping task involves copying, cutting, and pasting files between networked computers. Network Neighborhood makes this job easy by relying on familiar commands from the standard Edit menu.

To copy or move a file or folder from a networked computer to your hard drive, follow these steps:

1. Open the networked computer in the Network Neighborhood window.

2. Locate the file or folder you want to copy or move.

3. Select the file or folder. Choose Edit⇨Copy to copy the file or folder or Edit⇨Cut to move the file or folder.

4. Click the down arrow beside the text box in the Address bar, as shown in Figure 7-4, to access a list of available computers on the network.

5. Locate and choose your computer in the Network Neighborhood's computer listing. Select the folder you've chosen as the new home for your file and choose Edit⇨Paste.

You can easily reverse the process by moving your files to another networked computer. Just start out with your computer rather than with the networked computer. You can even move files from the computer two doors down from you to the computer in the den. The possibilities are endless.

Figure 7-4: Open your own computer's hard drive.

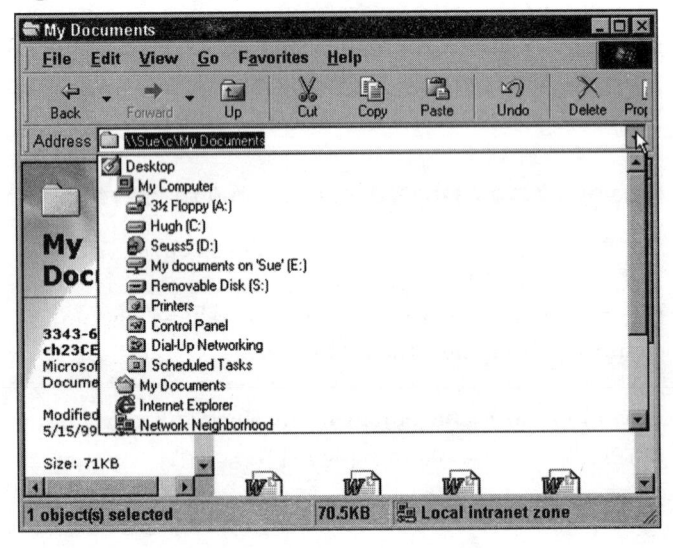

CHAPTER 8
PRINTING ON THE NETWORK

IN THIS CHAPTER

- Sharing a printer
- Installing a network printer
- Capturing a printer
- Managing the printer
- Getting the most out of your printer

Sharing a Printer

In Windows 98, you can share any printer attached to a computer on the network as easily as you share a drive or folder. You simply designate the printer as shared (with the access type you feel is appropriate) and assign it a share name, and your local printer is now a network printer available to all on the network. As you may expect, you can also set a password on the shared device so that only someone who knows the password can use the printer.

In addition to designating a printer as shared, you must make sure that you have installed your printer's driver on all other networked computers. The printer's *driver* is the software program that enables the computer to communicate with the printer. Without it, computers on the network will be blocked from using the network printer. Windows 98 makes it easy for you to install drivers over the network, so don't worry about that for now.

I am going to assume that somewhere on your network you have at least one computer with a local printer physically connected to it. Your mission (should you choose to accept it) is to designate that local printer for network use. Here's how:

1. Choose Start➪Settings➪Printers from the computer with the local printer. The Printers dialog box appears.

2. Right-click the printer's icon and choose Sharing from the pop-up menu that appears. The printer's Properties dialog box appears with the Sharing tab displayed.

3. Choose the Shared As option to display the share options, as shown in Figure 8-1.

Figure 8-1: Enter the share name and other information.

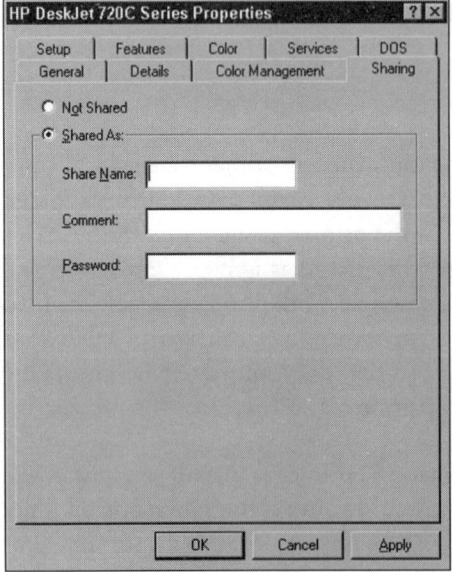

4. If Windows 98 suggests a share name, you can either accept that name or enter a new one. The share name is the name that displays in the Network Neighborhood window.

5. If you want, you can enter information about the printer in the Comment text box. Listing the brand name or whether it's a color printer may be helpful. The comment also appears in the Network Neighborhood window.

6. If you want to control the use of the printer, enter a password in the Password text box.

7. Click OK to accept the changes and close the Printers dialog box.

You can view a printer on the network via Network Neighborhood, Windows Explorer, or My Computer.

Installing and Configuring a Network Printer

The one printer physically attached to your computer will always act as that computer's local printer. The trick now is to get this local printer to act as the printer for all other computers on the network. Designating a printer as shared is the first step, but you still have to install the network printer on each of your networked computers. Luckily, managing this feat isn't so tricky after all, if you let Windows 98 do the work for you.

Installing a network printer

You use the same Add Printer Setup Wizard to install a network printer that you use to install a local printer. When you add a network printer to a printer-less computer on the network, however, the wizard copies the driver already installed on the computer with a printer and installs the driver to the printer-less computer for you. What's more, because you don't actually have a physical printer connected directly to the networked computer, you no longer have to bother selecting a port for the printer to use.

To install a network printer, follow these steps:

1. Choose Start➪Settings➪Printers. The Printers window appears.

2. Double-click the Add Printer icon. The first Add Printer Wizard dialog box appears, telling you that the wizard will help you install a printer.

3. Click the Next button to continue. The second Add Printer Wizard dialog box appears.

   At any time during the installation, you can click the Back button to review your choices.

4. Choose Network Printer and click the Next button. The next wizard dialog box appears, as shown in Figure 8-2.

Figure 8-2: Locate the network printer.

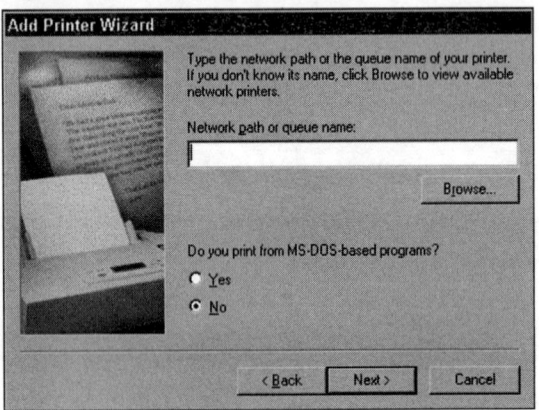

5. Enter the pathname for the network printer. If you don't know the pathname, you can use the Browse button to locate the computer for the network printer. If you then double-click the computer to which the printer is attached, you see a listing of attached printers. Figure 8-3 shows the Browse for Printer dialog box.

Figure 8-3: Select the printer.

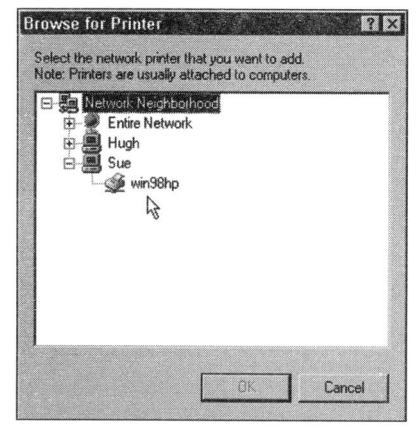

[Browse for Printer dialog box showing Network Neighborhood tree with Entire Network, Hugh, and Sue (expanded to show win98hp)]

6. Choose the printer and click OK. Click Next.

7. You can enter a new name for the printer or accept the default. Also, choose whether to make the printer the default for your computer. Click Next.

8. The wizard asks if you want to print a test page. You should always test the connection. The wizard sends a test page to the printer and asks if the page printed correctly. If the page printed, click Yes; if the page didn't print or had trouble printing, click No. If you click No, the wizard displays the Print Troubleshooter to help you solve the problem.

After you install the network printer, the printer's icon appears in the Printers window.

Configuring the printer

You can configure any network printer any way you want; those settings apply only to that printer on your computer. Changes you make to the networked printer's properties on your computer don't affect the printer's properties on any other computer.

You can configure the following options for a network printer by right-clicking the printer's icon in the Printers window. The pop-up menu that appears has these seven options:

- **Open:** Use this option to open the print queue. See the "Using the print queue" section later in this chapter for more information.

- **Work Offline:** Use this option if it makes sense to set up a number of print jobs without actually being connected (or *online*) with the printer. Maybe the computer attached to the printer isn't currently on, for example, but you still want to get your print jobs ready. You can then send them to the printer later, when the computer and printer are turned on.

- **Set as Default:** The most basic option you can set is whether the printer is your default printer or not. If you choose to make the printer your default, all applications on your computer automatically print to the default printer unless you specify a different printer with each job. If the Set as Default option is checked, the printer is set as the default printer. Clicking the option toggles this feature on or off.

- **Create Shortcut:** Use this option to create a printer shortcut. When you create the shortcut, the network printer appears on your desktop so you can print to it quickly and easily.

- **Delete:** Choose Delete if you want to remove the printer driver from your computer.

- **Rename:** Choose Rename to change the name of the printer on your computer. This option won't affect other computers on the network.

- **Properties:** Printer properties vary from printer to printer. Usually, you can change the paper size and orientation, set the resolution for graphics, or determine the type of fonts you want to use. If you're using a color printer, you may be able to set color options in the Properties dialog box (depending on the type of printer you own).

Capturing a Printer Port

Many MS-DOS applications and some 16-bit Windows programs will only print to an LPT (parallel) port. These programs cannot recognize a network path as it is normally written.

Capturing the printer port is the only way you can make the program recognize a network printer. It sounds very war-like, but in essence it's the same thing as mapping a drive. (For more information on mapping a drive, see Chapter 6.) By explicitly assigning the network printer path to a particular LPT port, you can force your MS-DOS applications and older Windows programs to print to the network printer.

To capture a printer port, follow these steps:

1. Right-click the printer's icon in the Printer's window and choose Properties from the menu. The Properties dialog box appears.

2. Choose the Details tab and then click the Capture Printer Port button. The Capture Printer Port dialog box appears, as shown in Figure 8-4.

3. In the Device drop-down list, choose the LPT port you want to assign to the capture.

4. In the Path text box, enter the network path to the printer.

Figure 8-4: Capture a printer port.

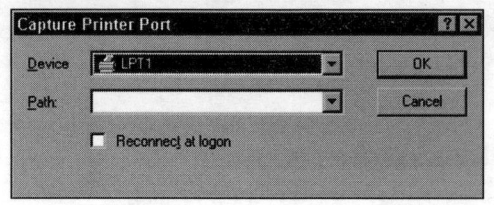

   5. If the program is one you use often and you want to reconnect this capture each time you log on to the network, check the Reconnect at Logon box.

   6. Choose OK and then OK again to close the printer's Properties dialog box.

Managing the Printer

When you have a local printer attached to your computer, you are the master. You control all aspects of your printing. You can pause printing, you can rearrange the order in which the documents print, or, if you like, you can even cancel printing a document on a whim.

When you print to a network printer not physically attached to your computer, all that power is taken away from you. All you can do is send your job to the printer and hope for the best. By using a network printer, you relinquish all control to the computer physically attached to the printer. To see what kind of control is involved here, look at the role of print queues in a networking environment.

Using the print queue

The *print queue* is an area in which all print jobs to a specific printer wait to be printed. The print queue holds the jobs so that you can get on with your work in Windows 98 while the network printer takes care of the printing chores. As the printer becomes available to print a job, the queue sends the jobs to the printer, one by one.

Usually, the print queue passes documents quickly to the printer. If several jobs are waiting in the queue or if there's a problem with the printer (out of paper, paper jam, or some similar catastrophe), the jobs wait in the queue until they can print. Depending on whether your computer controls the network printer or not, you may be able to use the print queue to manage some aspects of your printing jobs. Everyone, however, should be able to use the print queue to pause one of their printing jobs. This feature can be useful when you need to use special paper (such as a letterhead) for a printing job.

To open the print queue, open the Printers window and either double-click the Print icon or right-click the icon and then choose Open from the menu that appears.

Figure 8-5 illustrates a print queue that is paused so you can see the jobs waiting to be printed. Notice that four of the print jobs belong to one user (or owner, as the heading in the window shows) and one print job belongs to another user.

Figure 8-5: View the print queue.

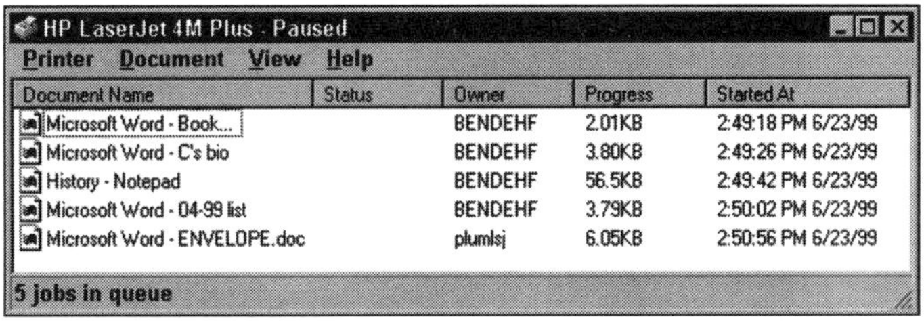
HP LaserJet 4M Plus - Paused
Printer Document View Help
Document Name Status Owner Progress Started At
Microsoft Word - Book... BENDEHF 2.01KB 2:49:18 PM 6/23/99
Microsoft Word - C's bio BENDEHF 3.80KB 2:49:26 PM 6/23/99
History - Notepad BENDEHF 56.5KB 2:49:42 PM 6/23/99
Microsoft Word - 04-99 list BENDEHF 3.79KB 2:50:02 PM 6/23/99
Microsoft Word - ENVELOPE.doc plumlsj 6.05KB 2:50:56 PM 6/23/99
5 jobs in queue

Obviously, you have complete control over your own local printer's queue. You, as the printer owner, can do with the printer queue what you want. If your computer happens to have the network printer attached to it, you have as much control over the printer queue as if it were just for your local printer. Be careful how you use this power, however. You can become very unpopular if you are seen as manipulating the printer queue for your own dark purposes. Following are the things you can do (or manipulate) when you control the network printer:

- You can pause jobs in the queue. You may want to change the printer's toner cartridge or insert special paper. To pause all print jobs, open the queue and choose Printer➪Pause Printing. A check mark appears beside the command on the menu. To release the paused print jobs, choose Printer➪Pause Printing again to remove the check mark.

- You can delete jobs from the print queue. You may want to delete the jobs in the queue to reset the printer. To delete all of the print jobs from the queue, open the queue. Choose Printer➪Purge Print Documents. All jobs are erased from the queue.

- You can pause the printing of one document. Suppose you really need that report to print immediately. Unless your job is first in the print queue, you have to wait. By using the power of the print queue, you can pause the printing of any document ahead of you in the queue and take your job to the head of the line. Simply open the queue and select the job you want to pause. Choose Document➪Pause Printing. A check mark appears beside the job and the word Paused appears in the Status area of the queue. You can pause any job ahead of yours in the queue. When your job is finished, you can continue printing any paused job by choosing Document➪Pause Printing again to remove the check mark.

- You can cancel one print job. If you want to cancel just one print job but let the others continue to print, you can select that job in the queue. Choose Document➪Cancel Printing. Don't abuse this power, because canceling other people's print jobs tends to annoy them.

You have much less control over your documents when you send them across the network to another printer, and you have no control over other users' documents on a network printer that isn't attached to your computer.

To see how weak you actually are in these situations, consider the following:

- You cannot change the order of the jobs in the print queue. You can't even change the order of your print jobs in the queue.
- You cannot restart a printer that has been paused.
- You cannot cancel all print jobs in the queue.

However, you can control a few small things when printing to a network printer that is not connected to your computer:

- You can pause the printing of one of your own print jobs. Simply select the job in the queue and choose Document➪Pause Printing. A check mark appears beside the command. To start printing the job again, select it in the queue and choose Document➪Pause Printing to remove the check mark from the command.
- You can cancel any of your own print jobs. To cancel one of your print jobs, select the job in the queue and choose Document➪Cancel Printing.

Optimizing Print Resources

You can do several things to optimize your printers and print services, whether the printer is a local or a network printer. Following are some things to think about:

- Consider the speed of the printer before you purchase it. For a home network, speed may not be a big concern; however, a network printer is used more often than a local printer, and a slow printer will slow down your network considerably.

- Make sure you have the correct printer driver for your printer. Using a substitute driver or a driver close to but not quite the driver you need may slow your printer. Use the manufacturer's driver if you can't find the right one in Windows 98. Also, if you have a new printer, consider downloading an updated driver version from the Internet for your printer.

- Network connections affect printing over the network. If your network is slow — 1 Mbps or less, for example — printing over the network will be slow too.

- Parallel port speeds are two to four times faster than serial ports. If possible, use parallel ports to attach printers to your computers.

- Keep your printer clean. Be careful when cleaning inside of the printer; some parts are delicate. Maintain a cool and consistent temperature around the printers as well, because some printer components are sensitive to environmental changes.

- Watch how you store your printer paper; for example, damp or wrinkled paper can damage your printer and cause frequent paper jams. Old paper, heavier paper than your printer can manage, and cheap paper or envelopes can also cause printer problems.

CHAPTER 9
MANAGING THE NETWORK

IN THIS CHAPTER

- Understanding network management
- Using NetWatcher
- Using WinPopup

Understanding Network Management

Managing your network should be an easy job with a peer-to-peer network. All you really need to do is make sure everyone on the network can access their files and all other network resources they need in order to do what they want to do.

Of course, you are likely to run into problems from time to time. Keeping a notebook log about your network makes managing the network easier. Include network maps, a list of each computer's resources, configuration settings, and other details that help you quickly and easily find any information about your network as you need it. Following is a partial list of information you should log about your computers and your network:

- For every computer on the network, list hardware and software; the operating system; the computer's manufacturer, model, and serial number; the monitor brand and specifications; keyboard type; mouse type; processor speed;

RAM amount and type; size and type of hard disks; and so on. This information is useful when you want to upgrade or locate problems with your computers.

- List protocols, IP address(es) if applicable, and other networking software information.

- List networking hardware — network cards, cabling, connectors, hubs, and so on. Include brands, types, identification numbers, and any other information you need. List other information, such as IRQs of network cards, and note each user's name and password for the network.

- List all drives, including sizes, brands, manufacturers, speeds, model, drivers, and so on — CD-ROM, Iomega Zip or Jaz drives, tape drives, and their shares (resources shared).

- List all peripherals: printers, modems, scanners, and other equipment. Give the manufacturer, model, and any specifications on memory, ports, and cables for each peripheral.

- List all applications on each computer, plus the licensing and sharing designations.

Keep all documentation in one area and keep a list of contact names and numbers for help, tech support lines, and so on. Keeping this information handy and up to date helps you with optimizing your network and troubleshooting problem areas.

Next, add to that log any problems you have and how you've fixed them. If you run into a problem with your network once, you'll likely run into it again at a later date. Having a log of those problems and solutions can help you later if the problem reoccurs.

Using NetWatcher

NetWatcher is a Windows 98 application you can use on a network to monitor shared resources. You can view each user attached to a computer and the folders and files they're using. You can also disconnect a user, close a file, add a shared folder, view the shares on your own computer and on other computers (if you have the password), and more. You can also perform tasks on a remote computer after you open it in NetWatcher.

Configuring the computer for NetWatcher

To use Netwatcher, you must first allow remote administration on all computers on the network. Allowing *remote administration* on a computer means that any user is able to create, change, and monitor shares on that computer. However, Windows 98 lets you assign a password to this process so that only a person who knows the password can perform the task. The person who knows the password can then monitor all other computers from any computer on the network.

To allow remote administration, follow these steps:

1. Choose Start⇨Settings⇨Control Panel. The Control Panel appears.
2. Double-click the Passwords icon in the Control Panel.
3. Choose the Remote Administration tab.
4. Check the Enable Remote Administration of This Server check box.
5. Enter the password and then enter it again to confirm it. As you enter the password, Windows 98 displays only asterisks to thwart those who might be looking over your shoulder.

6. Click OK. Repeat these steps on any other computers on the network you want to allow remote administration on.

In addition to allowing remote administration, you must allow file and print sharing, if you have not already done so. Open the Network icon in the Control Panel and click the File and Print Sharing button. Make sure both check boxes are checked. For more information, see Chapter 4.

Starting and quitting NetWatcher

When you start NetWatcher, any connections to your computer appear in the window. As additional users or connections are made, the window displays those connections as well. You can also update the view at any time to make sure all connections are showing. To open NetWatcher, choose Start⇨Programs⇨Accessories⇨System Tools⇨NetWatcher.

Figure 9-1 shows the NetWatcher monitoring a user on the network. The program lists the folders that are shared: the C drive, the Zip drive, and the color printer; it also shows two documents the other user has opened.

NetWatcher includes various tool buttons you can use to control it. Table 9-1 explains the tool buttons.

Table 9-1: NetWatcher Tool Buttons

Tool Button	Description
Select Server	Choose the computer you want to monitor. You must know the remote administration password.
Disconnect User	Disconnect any user from the selected share. The user will lose all unsaved data.
Close File	Close any shared file, even while the user is connected. The user will lose all unsaved data.

Chapter 9: Managing the Network

Tool Button	Description
Add Share	Designate a folder or resource as shared.
Stop Sharing	Designate a folder or other resource as no longer shared.
Show Users	Displays a view of connected users, their computer, the number of open shares and open files, the amount of time they've been connected, and the names of the shared folders.
Show Shared Folders	Lists the shared folders' paths, names, and access types. You can also view which computer is attached to each shared folder. See Figure 9-1 for the show shared Folders view.
Show Files	Lists the open files, the share used, and the user connected to the file. You can also see the access type of the open file.

To close NetWatcher, simply click the Close (X) button in the upper-right of the window.

Selecting a server

NetWatcher refers to all computers on the network as servers, even in a peer-to-peer network. The server, in this case, is the NetWatcher server software. You can view your own shared resources as well as other computers on the network, as long as you know the password set in the Remote Administration dialog box.

To select a server, follow these steps:

1. Open NetWatcher.

2. Choose Administer➪Select Server. The Select Server dialog box appears, as shown in Figure 9-2.

CliffsNotes Setting Up a Windows 98 Home Network

Figure 9-1: Use NetWatcher to view shares.

Select server
Disconnect User
Close File
Add Share
Stop Sharing
Show Users
Show Shared Folders
Show Files

Figure 9-2: Enter the server's name.

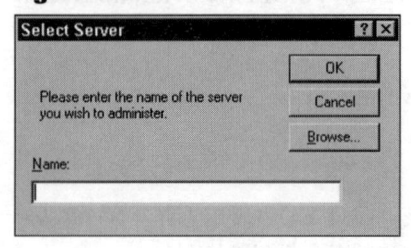

3. Enter the server's name or use the Browse button to locate the computer.

4. Click OK. The Enter Network Password dialog box appears.

5. Click OK. The selected server's shares appear in the NetWatcher window.

Remember: After you've accessed a server using the password, Windows adds it to your password list. You only have to enter the password once to access each server.

Disconnecting a user

You can disconnect a user from the server you're monitoring at any time. When you disconnect the user, however, you should make sure the user has closed all open files from that computer.

You can only disconnect a user in Show Users view.

To disconnect a user, click the Disconnect User button. A warning dialog box appears. Click Yes to continue. NetWatcher doesn't warn the user when you disconnect him or her.

Closing a file

As with disconnecting a user, you must be careful when closing a file in use. You should warn a user before you close the file so the user can save changes. If the user doesn't save changes, he or she will lose any unsaved data.

To close a file, select the Show Files view. Select the open file and click the Close File button. A warning dialog box appears. Choose Yes to close the file. Again, NetWatcher doesn't warn the user.

Working with shared folders

You can share folders on any server computer to which you're attached with NetWatcher. You can open any drive and share any folder; the remote administration password gives you the permission you need to perform these tasks.

To share a folder, follow these steps:

1. Open NetWatcher and the computer you want to monitor.
2. Change to the Shared Folders view.
3. Choose Administer➪Add Shared Folder. The Enter Path dialog box appears, as shown in Figure 9-3.

Figure 9-3: Share a folder.

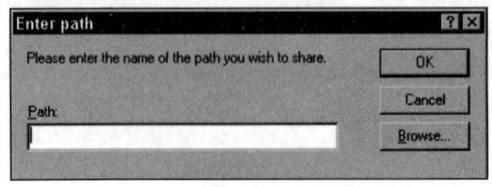

4. Enter the path or use the Browse button to locate the desired folder on the server computer.
5. Click OK. The Share dialog box appears.
6. Choose Shared As and enter the share name and access type.
7. Click OK to close the Share dialog box.

You can stop sharing a folder by selecting the folder and then clicking the Stop Sharing Folder button.

You can view a shared folder's properties by selecting the folder and choosing Administer➪Shared Folder Properties.

Using WinPopup

WinPopup is a Windows 98 program that enables you to chat with others on the network. You can send messages to one person or to all network users. You can also set options to play sounds or otherwise notify you when someone sends a message.

WinPopup is a simple program you can use to notify the others on the network, for example, that you have to disconnect someone from your computer or that the printer is turned off. You can even use WinPopup to announce that dinner is ready.

Locating WinPopup

No icon or program listing exists for WinPopup, but you can create a shortcut for the program in the Windows Explorer. WinPopup is located in the Windows directory.

Locate the program icon — winpopup, right-click it, and choose Create Shortcut from the pop-up menu that appears. You may also want to place WinPopup in your StartUp folder so that it starts automatically when you start your computer.

Sending messages

To use WinPopup, you must start the program and leave it running. For you to contact anyone on the network, that person must also be running WinPopup. You can minimize the window so that it doesn't interfere with your work.

You can send a message to one user by entering the user's name or the computer name. Alternatively, you can send the message to everyone on the network by entering the workgroup name.

CliffsNotes Setting Up a Windows 98 Home Network

To send a message, follow these steps:

1. Open the WinPopup window, as shown in Figure 9-4.

Figure 9-4: Open the WinPopup window.

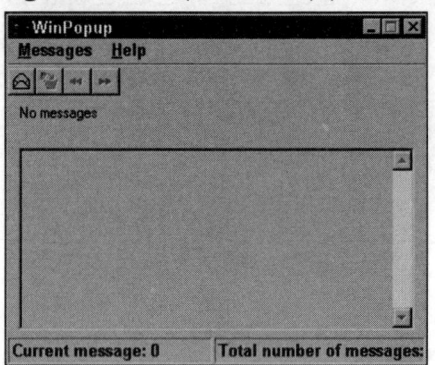

2. Click the Send button (the envelope). The Send Message dialog box appears, as shown in Figure 9-5.

3. In the To area, choose either the User or Computer option or the Workgroup option and then enter the appropriate user or workgroup name in the text box below the options. Choose multiple names if you want to send the message to more than one person.

4. Enter text in the Message area.

Figure 9-5: Create a message to send to network users.

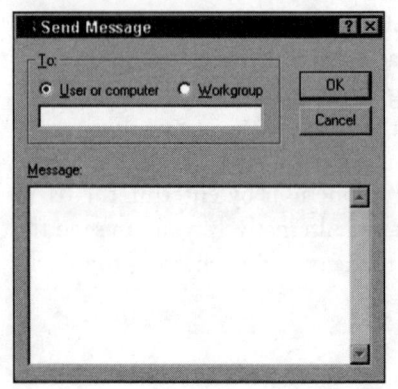

Chapter 9: Managing the Network

5. Click OK. WinPopup sends the message and displays a dialog box telling you the message was sent successfully.

6. Click OK. You can minimize the WinPopup window if you want.

Receiving messages

When you receive a message, the WinPopup window pops up on your screen, as shown in Figure 9-6. Notice that the sender sent the message to everyone on the network; the name of the workgroup is OPINIONS.

Figure 9-6: Send the message to everyone on the network.

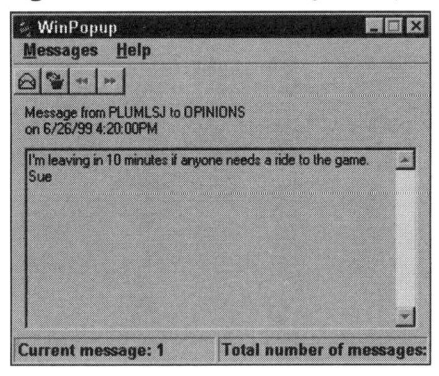

When you receive a message, you can choose to discard it by clicking the Delete button.

Changing options

You can change a few options in WinPopup. For example, you can change whether or not to play a sound when a new message arrives, whether to always display the WinPopup window on top of all other windows, and whether to pop up the window when you receive a new message.

To change options, choose Messages➪Options. The Options dialog box appears, as shown in Figure 9-7. Check (or uncheck) as many options as you like and then click OK when you're finished.

Figure 9-7: Select your options.

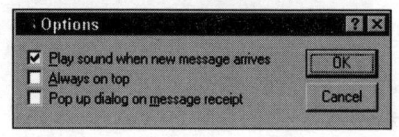

CLIFFSNOTES REVIEW

Use this CliffsNotes Review to practice what you've learned in this book and to build your confidence in doing the job right the first time. After you work through the review questions, the problem-solving exercises, and the fun and useful practice projects, you're well on your way to achieving your goal of setting up your own home computer network.

Q&A

1. Which of the following cannot be shared on a network?
   a. Files and folders
   b. CD-ROM drives
   c. Scanners

2. What type of network should you use if there are less than ten computers connected together? _____

3. Which of the following is the default networking protocol?
   a. TCP/IP
   b. NetBEUI
   c. IPX/SPX

4. Do you have to log off of the network before you shut down the computer? _____

5. Why do you map a drive? _____

Answers: (1) c. (2) Peer-to-peer network. (3) a. (4) No, shutting down the computer automatically closes resources and logs you off of the network. (5) To quickly access another computer, drive, and folder.

Scenario(s)

1. You have a lot of mapped network drives and it takes a long time to log on to the network. Most of the time, you don't need to connect to all of your mapped drives. You should _____ _____.

2. You want to network the printer attached to your computer. You should _____ _____.

3. You use a MS-DOS program that only sees an LPT port. You want to use a network printer to print documents from that program. You should _____ _____.

4. You have two computers that you want to connect so you can transfer files and share a printer; but you don't want to put a lot of money into a network. You should _____ _____.

Answers: (1) Choose Quick Logon in the Network dialog box. (2) Install the printer for network use and share the printer. (3) Capture the network printer to your computer. (4) Use a parallel or serial file transfer cable to connect the two computers.

Consider This

- Did you know that you can connect a laptop to your home network without using a network card and without installing networking software? Using direct cable connections, you can share files and printers on the network quickly and easily with a laptop computer. See Chapter 3 for more information.

- Did you know that you can protect personal or confidential files from others on the network and still share some files and folders on your computer? See Chapter 5 for more information about sharing and limiting access.

Practice Project

1. After you share some files and limit access to others, check another computer on the network to make sure you correctly shared your resources. Try to access files you did not share to make sure they are safe. See Chapter 5 for more information.

2. Locate the computer with the fastest CD-ROM on the network and share that drive. Place a CD-ROM — such as a game, map program, or encyclopedia — in the drive. Go to another computer on the network and open the CD in the other computer. Open the program or game and run it for at least 5 minutes to see how much faster the CD runs on the networked computer than it does on your own. See Chapter 5 for more formation about sharing.

3. Locate another computer on the network that has some extra disk space. Create a folder on that computer for your own files and folders. Map the network drive to that folder for quick and easy access whenever you need it. Open the folder using the mapped drive and save a file to it. See Chapter 6 for help.

CLIFFSNOTES RESOURCE CENTER

Ready for more? The CliffsNotes Resource Center shows you the best of the best — links to the best information in print and online. Here's some related information about setting up your Windows 98 network. You can also find help for working with Windows and the Internet and acquiring your networking equipment.

Books

This CliffsNotes book is one of many great books about computer networking in a Windows 98 environment by IDG Books Worldwide, Inc. So if you want some great next-step books, check out these publications:

Dummies 101: Windows 98. If you're looking for help with Windows 98 — such as instructions for using the operating system, ways of fixing problems with Windows, instructions on how to use the programs that come with Windows 98, and so on — Andy Rathbone is your man. He does an excellent job of explaining Windows 98 without relying on all the technical jargon. IDG Books Worldwide, $24.99.

Upgrading & Fixing PCs For Dummies, 4th Edition. Andy Rathbone can also help if you need to upgrade your current computers before adding Windows 98 or connecting them to a network. The author shows you how to install additional memory, a faster modem, adapter cards, and more. IDG Books Worldwide, $19.99.

Dummies 101: The Internet for Windows 98. Hy Bender and Margaret Levine Young provide a great resource for learning about all aspects of the Internet — the World Wide Web, e-mail, discussion groups, and so on. IDG Books Worldwide, $24.99.

Networking For Dummies, 4th Edition. Doug Lowe offers great tips and helpful advice to those interested in delving deeper into the world of computer networking. If you find your network growing, turn to Doug to help deal with the growing pains. IDG Books Worldwide, $19.99.

Quicken 98 for Windows For Dummies. If you're planning to use your computer and network for keeping your personal checking and savings accounts, Stephen Nelson can show you how to use the Quicken financial software package for retirement planning, investment management, and more. IDG Books Worldwide, $19.99.

It's easy to find books published by IDG Books Worldwide, Inc., in your favorite bookstores (on the Internet and at a store near you). We also have three Web sites that you can use to read about all the books we publish:

`www.cliffnotes.com`

`www.dummies.com`

`www.idgbooks.com`

Internet

Check out these Web sites for more information about computer networking:

ZDNet, `web-e7.zdnet.com/products/network-hwuser/`, is a great resource if you need help choosing hubs, cabling, or network interface cards. And if you want to find out more about sharing printers, using network e-mail, or acquiring additional networking software, ZDNet is the place to be.

Linksys, `www.linksys.com/default.htm`, can give you the latest information on links for phone lines or Ethernet networking products. Be sure to check them out.

Intel's AnyPoint Home Network, `www.intel.com/anypoint/home.htm`, provides tons of information about home networking basics (including technical explanations of networking products and examples of products).

WinGate, `www.wingate.com/contact.htm`, may be a good starting point if you're interested in using a software product to share an Internet account. WinGate offers one of the better-known Internet Share software products on the market.

3Com, `www.3com.com/news/4p_musical.html`, asks a very simple question: Have you ever wished you could listen to your favorite CDs in every room in the house? Their answer is: Use your home network! You can have instant access to your music collection from any point in your house with the help of 3Com's home networking products. Check out their Web site for more information.

Next time you're on the Internet, don't forget to drop by `www.cliffsnotes.com`. We created an online Resource Center that you can use today, tomorrow, and beyond.

Checklist

Following is a checklist of steps for installing your home network:

1. Set network goals. Determine which programs you need, how many computers you need on the network, and where computers and printers will be located in the house.

2. If needed, upgrade your computers to make sure they all have enough power, memory, and disk space to run Windows 98 efficiently. Install Windows 98 on each computer that doesn't currently run it. You can alternatively use Windows 95 on the computers in the network; you may notice, however, that Windows 95 does not perform exactly the way Windows 98 does.

3. Purchase any peripherals you want, such as printers, modems, and so on.

4. Determine the type of home network you want: Ethernet, phone line, or wireless. Purchase networking kits and any extra equipment you need for additional computers. Make sure you get a network interface card for each computer, adequate cabling, and a hub, if necessary.

5. Install the networking hardware.

6. Install and configure the networking software.

7. Share drives, files, printers, and other resources.

8. Install any programs, such as an Internet sharing program, on the computers.

9. Teach the rest of the family to use the network successfully.

Send Us Your Favorite Tips

In your quest for learning, have you ever experienced the sublime moment when you figure out a trick that saves time or trouble? Perhaps you realized that you were taking ten steps to accomplish something that could have taken two or you found a little-known workaround that gets great results. If you've discovered a useful tip that helped you network with Windows 98 more effectively and you'd like to share it, we, the CliffsNotes staff, would love to hear from you. Go to our Web site at www.cliffsnotes.com and click the Talk to Us button. If we select your tip, we may publish it as part of CliffsNotes Daily, our exciting, free e-mail newsletter. To find out more or to subscribe to a newsletter, go to www.cliffsnotes.com on the Web.

INDEX

A
access control, 53
Add/Remove Programs Properties dialog box, 30

B
Browse for Printer dialog box, 88

C
cabling
　10BaseT cable, 35
　adding computers, 20
　Category 5, 20
　Direct Cable Connect (DCC) networks, 29, 31
　Ethernet kits, 20
　installing, 35, 36, 37
　interference, 19, 21, 37
　network card connection, 23, 26
　parallel file-transfer cable, 29
　twisted-pair cable, 34
　Unshielded Twisted Pair (UTP), 20
Capture Printer Port dialog box, 91
CD-ROM drive sharing, 7
Client for Microsoft Networks Properties dialog box, 74
CliffsNotes Web site, 3
connectors, 22, 23, 35

D
Direct Cable Connect (DCC)
　boot order, 33
　cabling, 29, 31
　configuring, 30, 31, 32
　establishing connections, 33
　installing, 29, 30
　printers, 28
　speed, 28
　Windows 98 setup, 32, 33
Direct Cable Connection wizard dialog box, 31
Disconnect Network Drive dialog box, 73
disconnecting users, 103
drive mapping, 70, 71, 72, 73
drive sharing, 6, 61

E
Enter Network Password dialog box, 103
Ethernet, 18, 20, 21, 35
expansion slots, 22

F
File and Print Sharing dialog box, 32, 50
file sharing
　closing files using NetWatcher, 103
　defining network services, 50, 51
　designating shared files, 62
　finding files, 68, 69, 70, 81, 82
　introduced, 6
　managing using Network Neighborhood, 83, 84
　naming files, 11, 12, 13
　passwords, 56
　read-only access, 56
　shortcuts, 82, 83
　simultaneous use, 14
　storing shared files, 16

Find All Files dialog box, 81
Find dialog box, 75
folder sharing
  choosing folders to share, 57, 58
  designating shared folders, 59, 60, 61
  finding folders, 68, 69, 70, 77
  introduced, 6
  managing using NetWatcher, 104
  managing using Network Neighborhood, 83, 84
  naming folders, 11, 12, 13
  nesting folders, 13
  passwords, 56, 60
  read-only access, 56, 60
  setup, 60
  shortcuts, 82, 83
  sorting order, 12
  systems folders, 12, 57

G

Getting on the Internet, 3, 63
goal setting, 7, 8
guest computers, 30, 31

H

hard drive sharing, 6, 61
hardware conflict, 44
hardware requirements, 9, 10, 14
Home Phoneline Networking Alliance (HomePNA), 19
host computer, 30
hubs, 10, 20, 26, 27

I

Industry Standard Architecture (ISA), 23

Installation Completed Successfully dialog box, 41
Internet access sharing, 63, 64, 65
Internet Package Exchange/Sequenced Package Exchange (IPX/SPX), 46
Internet Protocol (IP) address configuration, 48
Interrupt Requests (IRQs), 44
IPX/SPX (Internet Package Exchange/Sequenced Package Exchange), 46
ISA (Industry Standard Architecture), 23

K

kits
  contents, 17
  Ethernet, 20, 21
  phone line networks, 19
  wireless networks, 21, 22

L

licensing, 15
LinkLocal, 48
log book, 97, 98
logging off, 68
logging on, 66, 73, 74, 75

M

Map Network Drive dialog box, 71
mapping networks, 9
messaging, 105, 106, 107
modem sharing, 63, 64, 65
monitoring shared resources, 99

Index

N

nesting folders, 13
NetBEUI (Network Basic Input Output System Extended User Interface), 46, 48
NetWatcher
  closing, 101
  closing files, 103
  computer configuration, 99, 100
  disconnecting users, 103
  folder sharing management, 104
  selecting server, 101, 103
  starting, 100
  viewing shares, 102
Network Basic Input Output System Extended User Interface (NetBEUI), 46, 48
Network dialog box, 32
network interface card (NIC)
  buying, 22, 23, 24
  cable connection, 23, 26
  connector compatibility, 22, 23
  installing, 24, 25, 26
  interrupt request (IRQ) setup, 44
  introduced, 10
  PCMCIA cards, 23
  slots, 23
  software configuration, 44, 45
  software installation, 40, 41, 42, 43
network management
  disconnecting users, 103
  monitoring shared resources, 99
  remote administration, 99, 100
  selecting server, 101, 102, 103
Network Neighborhood
  file management using, 83, 84
  finding files using, 81, 82
  folder management using, 83, 84
  opening, 78
  shortcut creation, 82, 83
  viewing shared resources, 78, 79, 80
network path, 69
network protocols
  checking if installed, 33
  installing, 47, 48
  IPX/SPX, 46
  NetBEUI, 46, 48
  TCP/IP, 43, 46, 48, 49
network services, adding, 50, 51
networked computers
  computer name, 33
  displaying shared resources, 76
  finding by name, 75, 76
  identifying to network, 33, 51, 52
  viewing using Network Neighborhood, 78
networked programs, 14, 15
networking software, 39, 43, 45
NIC. *See* network interface card (NIC)

P

passwords
  file passwords, 56
  folder passwords, 56, 60
  guest computers, 31
  NetWatcher server password, 103
  peer-to-peer network security issues, 67
  printer passwords, 87
  remote administration password, 99, 100
path name, 68, 69, 70
PCI (Peripheral Component Interconnect), 23
peer-to-peer networks, 6, 7, 67

Peripheral Component Interconnect (PCI), 23
Personal Computer Memory Card International Association (PCMCIA), 23
phone line networks, 18, 19, 37
planning, 9
Plug and Play cards, 40
popup messages, 105, 106, 107
ports
  hub ports, 20
  parallel ports, 29, 91, 96
  printer ports, 91, 92
  serial ports, 29, 96
  wireless ports, 38
Print Troubleshooter, 89
printer sharing
  canceling print jobs, 94
  changing printer properties, 90
  configuring shared printer, 89, 90
  default printer, 90
  defining network services, 50, 51
  deleting print jobs, 94
  designating local printer as shared, 85, 86, 87
  Direct Cable Connect (DCC) networks, 28
  drivers, 85, 87, 90, 96
  introduced, 7
  naming printer, 86, 89
  network printer installation, 87, 88, 89
  optimizing resources, 96
  passwords, 87
  path name, 88
  pausing print jobs, 94
  port capturing, 91, 92
  print queue, 92, 93, 94, 95
  remote printer control, 95
  removing printers, 90
  renaming printers, 90
  shortcut creation, 90
Printers dialog box, 86

Q

quick logon, 73, 74, 75

R

remote administration, 99, 100
Remote Administration dialog box, 101
Rideway, 64
RJ connectors, 35
Run dialog box, 69

S

Select Network Adapters dialog box, 42
Select Network Component Type dialog box, 41, 50
Select Server dialog box, 101
Send Message dialog box, 106
Share dialog box, 104
Sharing dialog box, 60
shortcuts, 82, 83
shutting down, 68
System Properties dialog box, 44

T

TCP/IP Properties dialog box, 49
Transmission Control Protocol/Internet Protocol (TCP/IP), 43, 46, 47, 48, 49
two computer networks, 28, 29, 30, 31, 32, 33, 34

U
username, 67

W
WinGate, 64
WinPopup, 105, 106, 107
WinProxy, 65
wireless networks, 21, 22, 38
workgroup name, 33

CliffsNotes

Your shortcut to success for over 40 years

Computers and Software
Confused by computers? Struggling with software? Let *CliffsNotes* get you up to speed on the fundamentals — quickly and easily. Titles include:

- Balancing Your Checkbook with Quicken®
- Buying Your First PC
- Creating a Dynamite PowerPoint® 2000 Presentation
- Making Windows® 98 Work for You
- Setting up a Windows® 98 Home Network
- Upgrading and Repairing Your PC
- Using Your First PC
- Using Your First iMac™
- Writing Your First Computer Program

The Internet
Intrigued by the Internet? Puzzled about life online? Let *CliffsNotes* show you how to get started with e-mail, Web surfing, and more. Titles include:

- Buying and Selling on eBay®
- Creating Web Pages with HTML
- Creating Your First Web Page
- Exploring the Internet with Yahoo!®
- Finding a Job on the Web
- Getting on the Internet
- Going Online with AOL®
- Shopping Online Safely